LONDON'S
MONUMENTAL WALKS

15 Walks Taking in the City's Best
Monuments, Statues & Memorials

npshire

D1240418

**CITY
BOOKS**

City Books • Bath • England

First published 2018

Copyright © Survival Books 2018
Cover design: City Books
Cover photo: Albert Memorial
Maps © Jim Watson

City Books, c/o Survival Books Limited
Office 169, 3 Edgar Buildings
George Street, Bath BA1 2FJ, United Kingdom
+44 (0)1305-266918
info@survivalbooks.net
www.survivalbooks.net and www.londons-secrets.com

British Library Cataloguing in Publication Data
A CIP record for this book is available
from the British Library

ISBN: 978-1-909282-95-7

Printed in China

Acknowledgements

The author would like to thank all the many people who helped with research and provided information for this book. Special thanks are due to Alex Browning for her invaluable research, Graeme & Louise Chesters and Richard Todd; Robbi Forrester Atilgan for editing; Peter Read for additional editing and proof-reading; Susan Griffith for final proof checking; John Marshall for DTP, photo selection and cover design; and Jim Watson for the superb maps.

Last, but not least, a special thank you to the many photographers – the unsung heroes – whose beautiful images bring London to life.

ACCESS

Most buildings and public spaces (e.g. parks) in London provide wheelchair access, but this doesn't apply to private buildings and gardens. Contact the relevant company or organisation if you have specific requirements. The Disabled Go website (www.disabledgo.com) provides more in-depth access information for many destinations.

Author's Notes

Please note the following regarding the walks in this book.

♦ **Length & Duration:** The length of walks is approximate – shown to the nearest quarter mile – as is the time required to complete them, particularly if you make a lot of stops (coffee, lunch, museums, shopping, etc.). The average walking speed is around 3mph but we have allowed for a much slower pace of just 2mph. (The idea isn't to get from the start to finish as quickly as possible!) You can, of course, start a walk from either end, combine a number of walks to make a longer walk, or alternatively, shorten a walk. Most walks are graded easy or moderate with relatively few steep hills or steps.

♦ **Opening Hours:** Most of the buildings and public spaces (e.g. parks) included in the walks are open seven days a week; opening times may vary for weekdays/weekends and by season. Most parks and gardens offer free access, unless otherwise indicated. The opening hours of many sights and museums (etc.) are listed, though these are liable to change. Where there's an entry fee, it's noted.

♦ **Transport:** All walks start and end at or near a tube or railway station. Most can also be reached by bus (routes aren't listed as there are too many to include them all) and sometimes by river ferry. The postcode of the starting point is shown should you wish to drive. However, the nearest car park or on-road parking may be some distance away, particularly in central London – and can be expensive. Also, walks don't always return to the starting point.

♦ **Maps:** The maps aren't drawn to scale. Points of interest are numbered. An overall map of London is included on pages 8-9, showing the approximate location of walks.

♦ **Food & Drink:** Recommended 'pit stops' have been included in all walks – shown in yellow in the map key and in the text (other food and drink places are numbered as landmarks but aren't specifically recommended). When not listed, a pub/restaurant's meal times are usually the 'standard' hours, e.g. noon-2.30 or 3pm and 6-11pm, although some are open all day and may also serve food all day (as do cafés). Many pubs are also open in the mornings for coffee and breakfast (etc). Telephone numbers are listed where bookings are advisable or necessary, otherwise booking isn't usually required or even possible. Note that in the City of London (the financial district), many establishments are open only from Monday to Friday. A rough price guide is included (£ = inexpensive, ££ = moderate, £££ = expensive); most recommended places fall into the inexpensive category.

Contents

John Betjeman, St Pancras Station

Introduction

It isn't perhaps surprising that in a city as rich in history as London, there's a wealth of public monuments, statues and memorials: in fact London probably has more statues than any other city in the world. Its streets, squares, parks and gardens are crammed with monuments to kings and queens, military heroes, politicians and local worthies, artists and writers, and notables from every walk of life, not to mention a few more controversial characters such as Oliver Cromwell and Arthur 'Bomber' Harris.

Many monuments celebrate great military victories such as Trafalgar or Waterloo, but there are also those that recall acts of courage by ordinary folk – like the plaques in Postman's Park – and a few which remember deeds perhaps best forgotten. Many subjects remain famous today – such as Prince Albert, who has the most impressive memorial in London – while others have faded from memory, but all have contributed to this great city and nation in some way and most are deserving of their place in history. As well as statues and monuments, we have also included magnificent fountains, wall reliefs and murals; the latter brighten up the walls of Fitzrovia and Soho.

London is also blessed with an abundance of abstract and contemporary works of art, which fire the imagination and add a touch of colour and surreal magic to its grey cityscape. Nowhere is this more so than in the City (the financial district, aka the Square Mile) – which has a long tradition of commissioning public works of art – where sculpture is an integral part of many new developments. The City is home to an annual 'Sculpture in the City' exhibition (www.sculptureinthecity.org.uk), when its streets are adorned with striking works from internationally renowned artists, while Regent's Park is the venue for the superb Frieze Sculpture Exhibition from July to October.

The walks in this book are between 2 and 6½ miles (3¼ to 10½ km) in length, averaging around 3½ miles (5½ km). However, it's best to allow half a day for the shorter walks and as much as a full day for the longer walks – particularly if you plan to partake of the many excellent pubs, restaurants and cafés along the routes (for your author, a good lunch is a prerequisite of a good walk!) – not to mention the many other diversions such as museums, galleries and churches.

Researching and writing *London's Monumental Walks* has been a fascinating and enjoyable journey. We hope you find them as entertaining and rewarding as we did; all you need is a comfortable pair of shoes, a sense of adventure – and this book.

David Hampshire
July 2018

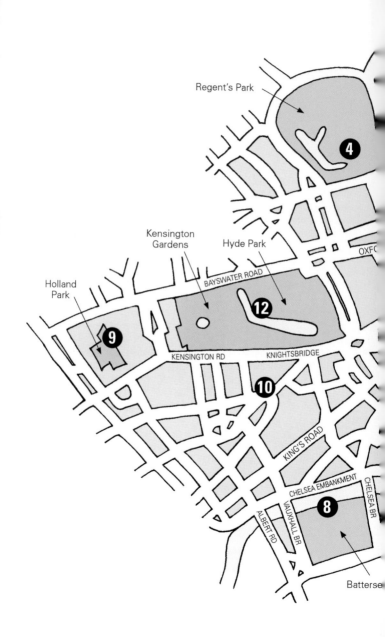

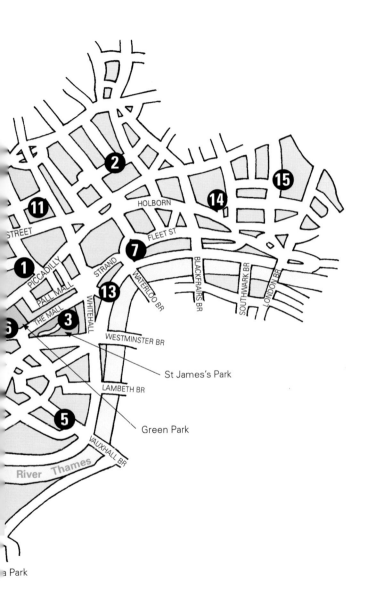

HOLBORN

FLEET ST

STREET

PICCADILLY

PALL MALL

STRAND

WATERLOO BR

BLACKFRIARS BR

SOUTHWARK BR

LONDON BR

THE MALL

WHITEHALL

WESTMINSTER BR

St James's Park

Green Park

LAMBETH BR

VAUXHALL BR

River Thames

a Park

END

Bond Street
tube

OXFORD STREET

51

DUKE STREET

STREET

NEW BOND ST

42

41

40

48 47 46
50
49

GROSVENOR ST

MOUNT STREET

45

BRUTON ST

43

44

DOVER STREET

OLD BOND ST

38
37
36

PICC

31

STAFFORD STREET

30

JER

39

KING

1 Eleanor Cross

2 Golden Springbok

3 Trafalgar Square

4 Nelson's Column

5 Bronze Lions

6 Charles I

7 Fourth Plinth

8 National Gallery

9 James II

10 George Washington

11 George III

12 St Martin-in-the-Fields

13 Café in the Crypt

14 Christ Child

15 Oscar Wilde

16 Edith Cavell

17 Sir Henry Irving

18 National Portrait Gallery

19 Leicester Square

20 Shakespeare Monument

21 Charlie Chaplin

22 Glockenspiel

23 Horses of Helios

24 Three Graces

25 Eros

26 St James's Square

27 William III

28 WPC Yvonne Fletcher

29 Classical Muses

30 Beau Brummel

31 Fortnum & Mason

32 St James's Piccadilly

33 Mary of Nazareth

⬤ Places of Interest   ⬤ Food & Drink

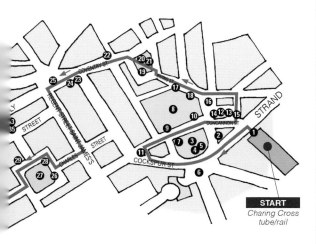

WALK 1

Trafalgar Square to Grosvenor Square

Distance: 3½ miles (5½ km)
Terrain: easy
Duration: 2-3 hours
Start: Charing Cross tube/rail
End: Bond Street tube
Postcode: WC2N 5DR

This walk begins in Trafalgar Square and explores the squares and spaces at the very heart of London – quite literally, as all distances from the capital are measured from here. One of the city's most prominent landmarks, Trafalgar Square commemorates the Battle of Trafalgar in 1805, a great British naval victory over the fleets of France and Spain off the coast

Admiral Nelson

of Cape Trafalgar in Spain. Not surprisingly, the square is where many of Britain's military heroes are commemorated, not least Admiral Horatio Nelson, shown left, who commanded the British fleet at Trafalgar.

From Trafalgar Square we visit Leicester Square – named after Leicester House, residence of the Earl of Leicester. This was a gentrified residential area in the 17th and 18th centuries, home to William Hogarth and Joshua Reynolds – both have statues in the square – but is now the centre of the city's entertainment quarter. From here it's a short hop to Piccadilly Circus – and its iconic statue of 'Eros'– and St James's, one of London's most affluent districts, noted for its gentlemen's clubs and upmarket boutiques.

From St James's we cross to exclusive Mayfair to visit the Royal Academy, Bond Street and Berkeley Square. The walk culminates in Grosvenor Square – the home of the official American presence in London from 1785 to 2017 (when the US Embassy moved south of the river) – which contains a number of statues and memorials to US leaders. From here it's a short walk to Bond Street tube station, our final destination.

TRAFALGAR SQUARE TO GROSVENOR SQUARE

Trafalgar Square to Grosvenor Square

Start Walking…

Leave Charing Cross station by the main exit onto the Strand. In the middle of the forecourt is the **Eleanor Cross** ❶, a 19th-century replica of a 13th-century structure built by Edward I (1239-1307) in memory of his wife Eleanor of Castile who died in 1290. There were 12 such crosses, marking the places her body rested on its journey from Lincoln to London; the last cross was the most ornate and is where Charing Cross derives its name from. The original cross was located at the top of Whitehall, where a statue of Charles I astride his horse now stands (see box).

From the station turn left along the Strand, where on the right-hand side at the end is South Africa House, which is adorned with a number of animal sculptures, including a leaping **Golden Springbok** ❷ on the corner of the building. Immediately in front of you is **Trafalgar Square** ❸ designed by Charles Barry and one of London's largest and most iconic squares, home to a

Statue of Charles I

This elegant statue was commissioned around 1633 by Richard Weston, Lord High Treasurer to Charles I, who planned to erect it in his garden at Roehampton, Surrey. It now stands facing down Whitehall towards Banqueting House, the place where its subject was executed in 1649. After the English Civil War the statue was sold to metal-worker John Rivett to be melted down, but he hid it until the Restoration in 1660. It was installed here in 1675 on the site where eight of the king's regicides – those who signed his death warrant – were themselves executed. The statue stands on the site of the last Eleanor Cross; a bronze plaque set in the pavement behind the statue marks the official centre of the city, from where all distances from London are measured.

wealth of statues and monuments. At the south side of the square is **Nelson's Column** ❹, the city's best-known monument, honouring Admiral Horatio Nelson (1758-1805) who defeated the French

Bronze Lion, Trafalgar Square

and Spanish fleets at the Battle of Trafalgar, but died at the moment of victory. Designed by William Railton and built between 1840 and 1843, the Corinthian column is 170ft (50m) high and is topped by an 18ft/5.5m sandstone statue of Nelson by Edward Hodges Baily, looking south towards the Admiralty. The square pedestal at the foot of the column is decorated with four superb 18ft^2 bas-relief bronze panels cast from captured French guns, depicting Nelson's most famous victories. Sir Edwin Landseer's four monumental **Bronze Lions** ❺ guarding the base of the column were unveiled in 1867, 24 years after the column was erected. Just behind the column, in the centre of the traffic island, is French sculptor Hubert Le Sueur's equestrian statue of **Charles I** ❻ (see box, page 13).

In front of Nelson's Column are four plinths, one in each corner. In the southwest corner is George Gammon's bronze of General Sir Charles Napier, installed in 1856 – Napier (1782-1853) is best known for his campaigns in India – while in the southeast corner is William Behnes' statue of Major General Sir Henry Havelock (1795-1857), who's famous for

the relief of Lucknow during the Indian Mutiny of 1857-9. On the plinth in the northeast corner is an exceptional equestrian statue of George IV (1762-1830) by Sir Francis Chantrey, installed in 1843. The **Fourth Plinth** ❼ (see box below), in the northwest corner, was originally intended for an equestrian statue of William IV, but the money ran out. Over the next 150 years there was much discussion about what to do with it (mustn't rush these things!), but it wasn't until 1999 that the decision was made to use it to display contemporary artworks.

Fourth Plinth

Many people wanted a permanent statue to occupy the fourth plinth, but the temporary occupants continue to amuse, inspire – and occasionally annoy. A sculpture of a (very) blue cockerel by Katharina Fritsch in 2013 led to controversy: a national symbol of France in a square celebrating a victory over that country! Other artworks to grace the plinth have included a golden rocking horse, Nelson's ship in a bottle, a bronze skeletal rider-less horse (shown) and a giant hand in a thumbs-up gesture (with a really long thumb).

On the north wall of the square, to the left of the George IV statue, are busts of three of Britain's greatest 20th-century naval heroes: (from left to right) Admirals Cunningham, Jellicoe and Beatty.

Trafalgar Square to Grosvenor Square

St Martin-in-the-Fields

St Martin-in-the-Fields

St Martin-in-the-Fields

One of London's most beloved churches, St Martin was designed by James Gibbs and completed in 1726 – and contains an abundance of memorials. In the church's portico is Mike Chapman's 1999 sculpture **Christ Child** 14, depicting a newborn baby that seems to emerge from a lump of rock; indeed, the baby's umbilical cord disappears into a 4.5-tonne block of Portland stone. In the southeast corner of the churchyard is the John Law Baker Memorial Drinking Fountain, a truncated fluted column with lion's-head fountains on two sides.

They were originally intended to stand at the centre of the fountains, but the Second World War intervened. The square's fountains also commemorate Beatty and Jellicoe: the western fountain is the Jellicoe Memorial Fountain and the eastern fountain the Beatty Memorial Fountain. The quatrefoil-shaped basins are by Charles Barry, though Lutyens added the vase-shaped central fountains; both contain fine bronze sculptural groups (mermaids, dolphins, sharks, etc.), the western fountain by Charles Wheeler and the eastern by William McMillan.

In the northwest corner of the square, on the lawn in front of the **National Gallery** 8, stands a fine bronze of **James II** 9 (1633-1701) – one of Britain's least popular monarchs – portrayed as a Roman emperor by Grinling Gibbons, who's widely regarded as Britain's finest wood carver. At the eastern end of the National Gallery (also on the lawn) is a bronze of **George Washington** 10

(1732-99), the first President of the United States of America; it's a replica of an original by Jean Antoine Houdon. Standing next to Washington is a column of 13 rods (or fasces), a symbol of power and strength through unity, which represent the founding states of the union.

Leaving the square via the southwest corner, walk along Cockspur Street and turn right into Pall Mall East, where there's a splendid equestrian statue of **George III** 11 (1738-1820) by Matthew Cotes Wyatt. Highly controversial in its day (George III was widely reviled), today it's a much-admired work, portraying the king astride his favourite horse, Adonis. Continue along Pall Mall East to the right, past the National Gallery to Duncannon Street, where on the left side stands **St Martin-in-the-Fields** 12 (see box above), home to the award-winning **Café in the Crypt** 13.

Continue along Duncannon Street and turn left down car-free Adelaide Street, where there's a striking memorial to **Oscar Wilde** 15

Edith Cavell

Celebrated for saving the lives of soldiers on both sides during the Great War, Edith Cavell (1865-1915) was a pioneer of modern nursing and was running a nurses' training school in Brussels when the Germans occupied Belgium. She was arrested in August 1915, accused of treason, court-martialled and sentenced to death. Despite international appeals for mercy, Cavell was executed by a German firing squad in October 1915, an act which received worldwide condemnation.

(1854-1900), writer, playwright and wit. The eccentric sculpture by Maggi Hambling – titled *A Conversation with Oscar Wilde* – was unveiled in 1998 and shows the head of Wilde (and a hand holding a cigarette – which has been stolen on several occasions) rising from a dark granite sarcophagus. The memorial is inscribed with one of Wilde's best quotes: 'We are all in the gutter but some of us are looking at the stars', from *Lady Windermere's Fan*.

Turn left at the end of Adelaide Street into William IV Street and St Martin's Place, where on the left there's a grand memorial to **Edith Cavell** 16 (see box above), a British nurse who became a reluctant heroine during the First World War. The Carrara marble statue by George Frampton was unveiled in 1920 and portrays Cavell in her matron's uniform beneath the inscription, 'For King and Country'. On top of the column is a sculpture of a woman and child, symbolising humanity, and on the back a British lion trampling on a serpent.

From St Martin's Place go right up Charing Cross Road where, on the north side of the National Portrait Gallery, is Thomas Brock's (1910) bronze of **Sir Henry Irving** 17 (1838-1905). A giant of the stage in the late 19th century (and the first actor to be knighted), Irving's statue is – surprisingly – the only thespian statue in central London, apart from that of Charlie Chaplin (see below). Established in 1856, the **National Portrait Gallery** 18 was the first of its kind in the world; the building was designed by Ewan Christian (in rather fanciful Florentine style) and opened to the public in 1896. The top of the façade, on both St Martin's Place and Irving Street, contains 18 medallions housing busts of artists and other notables, including Joshua Reynolds, William Hogarth, Louis-Francois Roubiliac, Peter Lely, Anthony Van Dyke and Hans Holbein the Younger (but no John Constable or JMW Turner!).

From the gallery take the first left down Irving Street to **Leicester Square** 19 , the heart of London's theatre district. Originally named Leicester Fields, the square was laid out in the 17th century by the Earl of Leicester. At the centre of the square is the **Shakespeare Monument** 20 by

(13) Café in the Crypt: A popular spot for breakfast, dinner and everything in between (hours vary, see www.stmartin-in-the-fields. org/visit/cafe-in-the-crypt, £).

(38) Royal Academy Grand Café: A relaxing setting for a snack, lunch or afternoon tea (daily, 10am-5.30pm, £).

(51) Selfridges: This supercool store has a wide choice of cafés, bars and restaurants, from the Italian rooftop 'alto' by San Carlo restaurant to the Hemsley+Hemsley café, Aubaine French bistro to the Champagne & Oyster Bar by Caviar House & Prunier (see www. selfridges.com/GB/en/ features/info/restaurants/ london-restaurantguide, £-££).

and is mounted on a pedestal flanked by dolphins at the centre of a fountain. Nowadays Leicester Square is synonymous with London's 'Theatreland', and is also where the latest blockbusters are premiered at one of the grand cinemas flanking the square. It's therefore appropriate that the final statue in the square is that of **Charlie Chaplin (21)** (1889-1977) by John Doubleday unveiled in 1981 – portrayed as the Tramp, his most famous role, with baggy trousers, derby hat and cane. Although he made his name in Hollywood, Chaplin was born in Walworth, south London.

From the square take the northwest (left) turning into Swiss Court to see the famous **Glockenspiel (22)**; originally attached to the front of the Swiss Centre (demolished in 2008), it was installed here in 2011 and sits atop a 'cantonal tree' displaying the coats of arms of the 26 cantons of Switzerland.

Giovanni Fontana, described by the art expert Nikolaus Pevsner as 'the most unpretentious monument that a capital has ever put up to their greatest national poet'. The marble figure – after an original by Peter Scheemakers in Poets' Corner in Westminster Abbey – was unveiled in 1874

Shakespeare Monument

Walk 1

Horses of Helios

Continue along Coventry Street, where on the left (opposite Great Windmill Street, home of the celebrated Windmill 'we never closed' Theatre) is the stunning **Horses of Helios** 23 statue and fountain. The bronze sculpture by Rudy Weller was installed in 1992 and depicts the four horses of Helios – Aethon, Eos, Phlegon and Pyrois – Greek God of the Sun. High above the statue, diving from the roof of the Criterion building, are the beautiful **Three Graces** 24, aka the Daughters of Helios; also by Rudy Weller (1992), it's made of aluminium covered in gold leaf. A few steps further on you come to Piccadilly Circus, home to one of London's most beloved landmarks, the statue of **Eros** 25 (see box), in front of the Criterion Theatre.

From the Circus head down Regent Street Saint James's

(renamed in September 2014) and take the third right into Charles II Street, which leads to **St James's Square** 26 (garden, Mon-Fri 10am-4.30pm). The only square in the exclusive St James's district, it was built after the restoration of Charles II in 1660 and is flanked by predominantly Georgian and Neo-Georgian architecture. In the centre of the garden is an equestrian bronze of **William III** 27 (1650-1702) by John Bacon (father and son), erected in 1808. The statue portrays the king as a Roman general and, unusually, includes a small molehill under the left rear hoof of the horse. The king died of pneumonia, a complication arising from a broken collarbone he suffered after a fall from his horse, Sorrell, which had stumbled on a molehill. Due to the mole's 'contribution' to the king's

Eros

Officially named the Shaftesbury Memorial Fountain, Eros was unveiled in 1893. The fountain commemorates the philanthropy of Lord Shaftesbury (1801-1885) and is topped by Alfred Gilbert's statue of a winged nude archer. The statue – the first made entirely of aluminium – is an icon of London, even being used as the symbol of London's *Evening Standard* newspaper, but it's actually misnamed. It's popularly thought to depict Eros, the Greek god of sexual love, but it's actually Anteros, his twin brother, the Greek god of selfless love.

Three Graces

demise, his Jacobite opponents fondly toasted the health of 'the little gentleman in the black velvet waistcoat'. In the southwest corner of the square is a bronze stag by Marcus Cornish, installed in 2001, while in the northeast corner (outside the square) is a memorial to **WPC Yvonne Fletcher** 28 (1958-1984), who was fatally shot by someone in the Libyan People's Bureau building (embassy) opposite. On the rooftop of 11 St James's Square, northwest of the square, are four **Classical Muses** 29 – goddesses of music, poetry, the arts and science – while next door (number 10) is Chatham House, former home of Prime Minister William Pitt the Elder.

Beau Brummell

From the square, take the western exit to King Street and turn right into Duke Street St James's and go left along Jermyn Street, where outside the entrance to Piccadilly Arcade (on the right) is a fine statue of **Beau Brummel** 30 (1778-1840). A dandy and close friend of the Prince Regent (later George IV), he was the greatest celebrity of his day, but fell from favour when he famously asked the person standing next to the prince, 'Who's your fat friend?' Reckless spending and gambling debts forced him to flee to France, where he died penniless. The statue, by Czech sculptor Irena Sedlecká, was unveiled in 2002.

Fortnum & Mason clock

Walk through the arcade to Piccadilly (if closed, return to Duke Street St James's and turn left). On the right is the Queen's favourite store, **Fortnum & Mason** 31 , founded in 1707, which has a splendid external clock. The ornate clock plays a selection of airs on 18 bells every 15 minutes, but the main event takes place on the hour when 4ft-high models of the store's two founders emerge and bow to each other, accompanied by chimes and 18th-century music. Continue east along Piccadilly to **St James's Piccadilly** 32 , a majestic Anglican parish church designed by Sir Christopher Wren and consecrated in 1684. The church's interior is worth a look, as it includes a superb reredos by Grinling Gibbons, but you're here to see the statues in the church's garden. These include **Mary of**

St James's Piccadully

Nazareth ㉝ by Charles Wheeler (ca. 1925), erected in 1975; **Peace** ㉞ by Alfred Frank Hardiman (ca. 1926); and, also by Hardiman, a memorial fountain to **Julius Salter Elias** ㉟ (1873-1946), 1st Viscount Southwood, a British newspaper proprietor and Labour politician.

Cross to the north side of Piccadilly and go west to the **Royal Academy of Arts** ㊱ (entry fee, 10am-6pm, 10pm Fri – see box right) located in Burlington House, one of London's finest Palladian buildings. The splendid reliefs around the entrance porch are by John Birnie Philip and date from 1874. The Royal Academy (RA) is an independent institution run by eminent artists to promote the creation and appreciation of visual arts. It was founded in 1768 by George III to educate, encourage and exhibit work by contemporary British artists; at the time fashionable taste leaned

towards traditional and continental art, and home-grown artists had little chance to shine. Visitors are greeted by Alfred Drury's theatrical bronze of **Sir Joshua Reynolds** ㊲ (1723-1792), a leading portrait painter and the RA's first president, situated in the courtyard in front of the Academy.

On the second floor level on the façade of Burlington House is an eclectic collection of statues, which include (from left to right) Phideas (the greatest ancient Greek sculptor) by Joseph Durham; Leonardo by Edward Stephens; Flaxman (the eminent English sculptor) and Raphael, both by Henry Weekes; Michelangelo and Titian by William Calder Marshall; Sir Joshua Reynolds and Wren by Edward Stephens; and, bizarrely, William of Wykeham (1320-1404), also by Durham. Wykham was a medieval Bishop of Winchester, Chancellor of England and founder of New College (Oxford) and Winchester College – but not an artist. Below, at either end of the ground level arcade, are two poignant war memorials: to the west is Trenwith Wills' Royal Academy Memorial

---

Michelangelo at the RA

The Academy has a vast collection of exhibits, but among the most cherished and charming is Michelangelo's *Taddei Tondo*, displayed in a purpose-built area on the Sackler Gallery landing. Created in Florence in 1504-06, it's the only marble work ((relief) by Michelangelo in the UK, and depicts the Virgin Mary and Child with the infant St John the Baptist.

Trafalgar Square to Grosvenor Square

Royal Academy of Arts

and to the east Geoffrey Webb's Artists Rifles Memorial. If you're peckish, the **RA Grand Café** 38 is a good place to stop.

From the RA go right on Piccadilly and some 150m along turn right down Dover Street, where on the left-hand corner in front of Caffè Nero is Elizabeth Frink's (1974) bronze **Horse and Rider** 39 , described by Frink as 'an ageless symbol of man and horse'. Continue along Dover Street and turn right down Stafford Street and left at the end on Old Bond Street. Around 100m along, soon after Old Bond Street becomes New Bond Street – near Asprey the jewellers – there's the superb bronze, **Allies** 40 (see box).

At number 153 New Bond Street, look up to see four **Abstract Pieces by Henry Moore** 41 , which form a screen that adorns the Time and Life Building (the address is actually 1 Bruton Street). The four external Portland stone works (1952) are in a Cubist style. Like Picasso (whom Moore had met), Henry Moore was fascinated by African and Oceanic art, which can be seen in the angular, bulky figures depicted in this work. At number 34-35 New Bond Street, embedded above the entrance of Sotheby's auction house, is London's oldest outdoor statue: the ancient Egyptian black basalt **Effigy of Sekhmet** 42 , the warrior goddess of Upper Egypt. Depicted as a lioness (the fiercest hunter known to the Egyptians), she was also a solar deity, bearing the solar disk and the uraeus (an upright form of spitting cobra). The statue dates from between

Allies

This much-loved and photographed statue by American sculptor Lawrence Holofcener, depicts Roosevelt and Churchill sitting on a bench and chatting amiably; it was financed by the Bond Street Association in 1995 to mark 50 years of peace. Churchill's mother was American and he and Roosevelt were distant cousins. After the war they helped to found the United Nations.

1600BC and 1320BC, and has been Sotheby's mascot since the 1880s, when it was sold at auction for £40 but never collected by the buyer.

Woman of Samaria

Retrace your steps to Bruton Street, turn right and continue to **Berkeley Square** ㊸, which was laid out in the mid-18th century by William Kent. The square's gardens are open to the public (unrestricted) and contain a solitary statue, albeit an important one; variously described as the Fountain Nymph, the Lansdowne Fountain and the **Woman of Samaria** ㊹, the Carrara marble statue is by Pre-Raphaelite sculptor Alexander Munro and dates from 1881. It depicts a semi-draped woman carrying a vase from which water pours to form a fountain. From the square, head north along its western edge and go left along Mount Street into Carlos Place, where there's an unusual fountain, **Silence** ㊺, by Japanese architect Tadao Ando, installed in 2011. The fountain contains two trees in a granite-edged pool; atomisers at the base of the trees create clouds of water vapour for 15 seconds every 15 minutes (glass lenses below the surface contain fibre optics that illuminate the basin at

night). The fountain is a memorial to Sir Simon Milton (1961-2011), a former leader of Westminster City Council.

Continue along Carlos Place to **Grosvenor Square** ㊻ (8am to dusk), London's second-largest garden square. It takes its name from Sir Richard Grosvenor (1689-1732), 4th baronet, an ancestor of the modern Dukes of Westminster, who developed the area in the early 1700s. Dubbed 'Little America', the square was – until 2017 – the home of the official American presence in London since John Adams (1735-1826) established the first American mission to the Court of St James's in 1785. Adams lived from 1785 to 1788 in a house that still stands on the corner of Brook and Duke Streets. The square is dominated by Eero Saarinen's monolithic US Embassy building, which is to become a luxury Rosewood Hotel (the US Embassy moved to Nine Elms in south London in 2017).

The square contains a number of significant statues and memorials, including a notable statue of **President Franklin Delano Roosevelt** ㊼ (1882-1945) by Sir William Reid Dick, unveiled by his widow in 1948. FDR is depicted standing on a plinth of Portland stone wearing a long cloak and leaning on a stick, a symbol of the illness from which he suffered most of his life that left him paralysed from the waist down. He was the longest serving US president in history – from 1933 to 1945 – and the only president to serve more than two terms due to the Second

Trafalgar Square to Grosvenor Square

World War. Other statues in the square include American Robert Lee Dean's bronze of **President Dwight D. Eisenhower** ④⑧ (1890-1969) in the northwest corner – Eisenhower had his wartime HQ at 20 Grosvenor Square – and a 10ft (3m) bronze of **President Ronald Wilson Reagan** ④⑨ (1911-2004) by American Chas Fagan, in the southwest corner. On the south side of the square is the Eagle Squadrons Memorial (1986) – surmounted by a bronze eagle by Elisabeth Frink – commemorating the American and British pilots who served in the RAF Eagle Squadrons in the Second World War. There's also a **September 11 Memorial Garden** ⑤⓪ (see box) to the Britons who died in the 9/11 terrorist attacks.

> ### September 11 Memorial Garden
>
> Grosvenor Square features a memorial to the 67 Britons who died in the 11th September 2001 attacks on the World Trade Centre and Pentagon in 2001. It consists of a small garden, featuring plants that are at their best in September, with a pavilion and pergola.

Exit the square in the northeast corner into Duke Street, walk to the end to reach Oxford Street. Opposite is **Selfridges** 51 department store, which contains a wealth of eateries, or turn right to reach Bond Street tube station around 100m further along.

September 11 Memorial Garden, Grosvenor Square

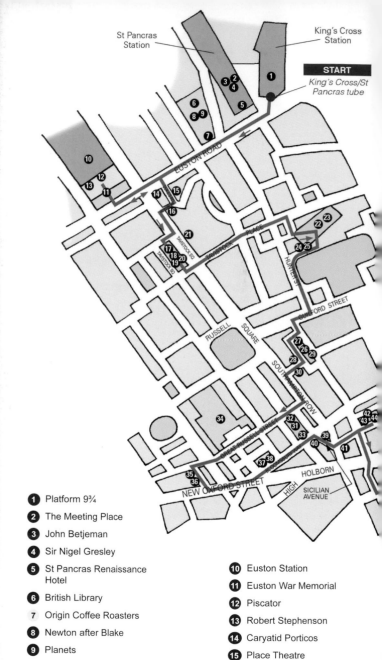

START
King's Cross/St
Pancras tube

St Pancras
Station

King's Cross
Station

EUSTON ROAD

TAVISTOCK SQ

TAVISTOCK SQ

TAVISTOCK PLACE

HUNTER ST

GUILFORD STREET

RUSSELL SQUARE

SOUTHAMPTON ROW

GREAT RUSSELL STREET

NEW OXFORD STREET

HOLBORN

SICILIAN AVENUE

HIGH

1. Platform 9¾
2. The Meeting Place
3. John Betjeman
4. Sir Nigel Gresley
5. St Pancras Renaissance Hotel
6. British Library
7. Origin Coffee Roasters
8. Newton after Blake
9. Planets
10. Euston Station
11. Euston War Memorial
12. Piscator
13. Robert Stephenson
14. Caryatid Porticos
15. Place Theatre
16. Woburn Walk

● Places of Interest ○ Food & Drink

WALK 2

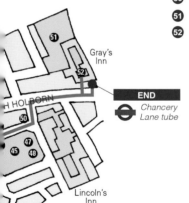

King's Cross to Chancery Lane

Distance: 4 miles (6½ km)
Terrain: easy
Duration: 2-3 hours
Start: King's Cross/St Pancras tube/rail
End: Chancery Lane tube
Postcode: N1 9AL

B rilliant Bloomsbury is the city's intellectual and literary quarter, home to many of its cultural, educational and healthcare institutions, from University College London to the British Museum and Great Ormond Street Hospital. Such is its reputation for cerebral celebrity, it often seems like every other house in Bloomsbury has a blue plaque to an eminent writer, scientist or philosopher, and its squares feature numerous statues and monuments.

The area has no official boundaries, but can be roughly defined as the 'square' enclosed by Tottenham Court Road to the west, Euston Road to the north, Gray's Inn Road to the east, and High Holborn to the south. Our walk starts at its northernmost point, at the regenerated King's Cross St Pancras hub – King's Cross is the home of the *Flying Scotsman* and Harry Potter's fictional Platform 9¾, while neighbouring St Pancras is the terminus for Eurostar services to the continent – and continues along Euston Road, taking in the British Library and Euston Station on the way.

We then head south to visit some of Bloomsbury's finest buildings and glorious garden squares (most gardens allow free access from dawn to dusk), the depository of a wealth of fine memorials and sculptures. Many streets and squares here are named after members of the Russell family (the Dukes of Bedford) who, along with the 4th Earl of Southampton (Lord High Treasurer to Charles II), developed the area in the 17th and 18th centuries; it was they who made Bloomsbury fashionable, and their influence can still be seen today.

The final leg of the walk strays into Holborn to visit Lincoln's Inn Fields – home to Sir John Soane's amazing museum – and Gray's Inn, before terminating at Chancery Lane tube station.

King's Cross to Chancery Lane

Start Walking…

Our walk starts at King's Cross St Pancras tube station, which serves two of London's most magnificent mainline stations: King's Cross and St Pancras. King's Cross underwent a £500m restoration between 2007 and 2012 and now has a new concourse with a striking white steel roof, said to be the longest single-span station structure in Europe. But a much smaller metal object is one of the station's main claims to fame. As every Harry Potter fan knows, Harry catches the Hogwarts Express from platform 9¾ at King's Cross, which is accessed by dashing through a brick wall between platforms 9 and 10. As a tribute to Harry, there's a **Platform 9¾ ❶** marked on the wall in the station concourse, with a luggage trolley embedded in the wall.

The Meeting Place

Just across Pancras Road, St Pancras is London's most majestic railway terminus, designed by William Henry Barlow and opened in 1868. St Pancras International (as it's now known) underwent a

---

St Pancras Renaissance Hotel

The St Pancras Renaissance Hotel occupies the lower floors of the former Midland Grand Hotel (1873-1935) – once dubbed London's most romantic building – including the main public rooms and 38 original bedrooms and suites. The original Midland Grand Hotel – designed by the prolific architect Sir George Gilbert Scott and opened in 1873 – was all about romance, grandeur and style. Today, the glorious Gothic Revival metalwork, gold leaf ceilings, hand-stencilled wall designs and grand staircase are as dazzling as the day it first opened. Sir John Betjeman called this Gothic treasure 'too beautiful and too romantic to survive in a world of tower blocks and concrete'. Its survival is a triumph that will take your breath away.

---

major redevelopment between 2004 and 2007, at the cost of £800m, and is crowned by another magnificent roof, containing some 2½ acres of glass, equal to almost two football pitches!

There are two much-loved sculptures within the station, both installed in 2007. Located on the Grand Terrace is Paul Day's work, **The Meeting Place ❷** – aka The Lovers – a 30ft (9m) bronze depicting a couple in an embrace. The second sculpture is Martin Jennings' magnificent 8.5ft (2.6m) statue of poet **John Betjeman ❸** (1906-1984) – a splendid tribute to the

John Betjeman

Walk 2

St Pancras Station

The famous St Pancras International Clock, reconstructed by the original makers Dent hangs high in the apex of Barlow's majestic railway shed. A more recent addition (on the Western Concourse) is Hazel Reeves' 2016 statue of railway engineer **Sir Nigel Gresley ④** (1876-1941), designer of the legendary steam locomotives *Flying Scotsman* and *Mallard*.

man who was largely responsible for saving the station from demolition in the '60s (along with numerous other buildings). The statue shows Betjeman looking up at the magnificent roof (or perhaps the train timetable?), and perfectly captures his character and persona.

And at the front of the station is one of its greatest treasures: the glorious façade of the gracious old Midland Grand Hotel, reincarnated in May 2011 as the splendid **St Pancras Renaissance Hotel ⑤** (see box, page 27).

From St Pancras, head west along Euston Road to another imposing building, the **British Library ⑥** , designed by Colin St John Wilson and opened in 1998. It's the UK's national library with over 14 million books, along with substantial holdings of manuscripts and historical items dating back to 2000BC. The **Origin Coffee Roasters 7** at the front of the library is a good spot for a caffeine shot (there are more food and drink options inside the library). Displayed on a high plinth in the piazza is Eduardo Paolozzi's huge bronze of **Newton after Blake ⑧** (see box).

Also located in the piazza is Anthony Gormley's **Planets ⑨** , comprising eight boulders with incised human forms placed on plinths around a circular space.

Newton after Blake

The 1995 sculpture is based on a 1795 print by William Blake (1757-1827) titled *Newton: Personification of Man Limited by Reason*, which depicts a naked Isaac Newton (1642-1727) sitting on a ledge beside a mossy rock face, while measuring with a pair of dividers; Blake intended the print to criticise Newton's profane knowledge. In the sculpture, the brilliant scientist resembles a mechanical object, with bolts at the shoulders, elbows, knees and ankles.

According to Gormley, his 2002 work 'celebrates the dependency of the body on the material world in this library, which is the repository of the fruits of the mind'. The positioning of the plinths makes an orbit that fits into the architectural setting, while the human forms are visible from a central point inside the circle.

From the library, continue along Euston Road, passing the handsome Euston Fire Station (1902, Grade II* listed) on the corner of Eversholt Street, to **Euston Station** ❿ and, just in front, Euston Square Gardens. In the centre of the gardens is the imposing **Euston War Memorial** ⓫ by Reginald Wynn Owen, dedicated to the men of the London and North Western Railway (LNWR) Company who died in the two World Wars. On the station forecourt, between the war memorial and the station, is **Piscator** ⓬, aka the 'Euston Head', a large abstract work (1980) by Eduardo Paolozzi named for the German theatre director Erwin Piscator. On the west side of the forecourt is a bronze statue of **Robert Stephenson** ⓭ (1871) by Carlo

Robert Stephenson

Marochetti. Robert Stephenson (1803-1859) was the only son of George Stephenson (1781-1848), the 'Father of Railways'. Robert Stephenson was chief engineer of the LNWR – which built the first main railway line into London – and, along with Isambard Kingdom Brunel, was one of Britain's two greatest Victorian railway engineers.

Cross Euston Road and turn left to St Pancras New Church on the corner of Upper Woburn Place. A beautiful Greek revival building, it was the most expensive church of its day when consecrated in 1822. At the east end, guarding the entrance to the crypt, are

British Library

Walk 2

two **Caryatid Porticos** 14 – sculpted female figures that serve as an architectural support, replacing a column or pillar – by Charles Rossi, a sculptor of Italian descent. When the caryatids arrived at the church they were found to be too tall and a section had to be cut from their midriffs, as a result of which they're rather dumpy and lack the elegance of the Greek originals from which they're copied (the originals support a porch on the Erechtheion, a 5th-century BC temple on the north side of the Acropolis in Athens). In the churchyard on the south side is Emily Young's head representing Archangel Michael the Protector, installed in 2005 in memory of the victims of the 7th July 2005 London bombings.

Just past the church turn right down Duke's Road where, on the left, is the **Place Theatre** 15, which has an attractive terracotta façade featuring a medallion of Mars and Minerva by Thomas Brock above the door. This is the insignia of the Artists Rifles (38th Middlesex Rifle Volunteer Corps) which became the 20th Middlesex Rifle Volunteers in 1880, as indicated below the medallion. Opposite are some elegant stuccoed houses with bowed shop fronts by Thomas

Mahatma Gandhi

Woburn Walk

Designed by Thomas Cubitt in 1822 as a shopping street, both sides of the walk have attractive low terraces of well-preserved, bow-fronted shops, painted black at ground-floor level and cream above. Today, it's a delightful pedestrianised street with antiquated street lamps, which add to its decidedly Dickensian character. There's a blue plaque on one of the houses in the block numbered 1-7, recalling that poet W. B. Yeats lived there from 1895-1919.

Cubitt, which continue around the right-hand corner into **Woburn Walk** 16 (see box). At the end of Woburn Walk turn left into Upper Woburn Place and carry on to **Tavistock Square Gardens** 17.

Dating from 1825, Tavistock is one of Bloomsbury's wealth of lovely squares and its layout of London planes and lawns is typical of many city squares. What sets it apart is the large number of memorials, which include Fredda Brilliant's bronze of **Mahatma Gandhi** 18 in the centre of the gardens, unveiled by Prime Minister Harold Wilson in 1968, and a bust of writer **Virginia Woolf** 19 (1882-1941), cast from a sculpture by Stephen Tomlin and erected by the Virginia Woolf Society in 2004; Woolf lived at number 52 (destroyed in the Blitz) on the south side of the square for 15 years. Another memorial is an unusual double bronze bust of **Dame Louisa Brandreth Aldrich-Blake**  (1865-1925), one of the UK's first female surgeons; the bronze is by Arthur George Walker and the plinth by Sir Edwin Lutyens. The gardens are also home to Hugh Court's Conscientious Objectors' Commemorative Stone, a massive slate stone located on the north side of the gardens, dedicated to 'all those who have established and are maintaining the right to refuse to kill', and a cherry tree planted in 1967 in memory of the victims of the Hiroshima and Nagasaki nuclear bombs.

On the east side of the square, in the private courtyard of Sir Edwin Lutyens' BMA House – home to the British Medical Association HQ since 1923 – are four large statues by James Woodford and Stephen Rowland Pierce, representing **Sacrifice, Cure, Prevention and Aspiration** , positioned around a pool. The gates, also by Lutyens, commemorate medical officers killed in the Great War. From the square turn left along Tavistock Place and take the fifth turning on the right down Wakefield Street to **St George's Gardens** , once the burial ground for two nearby churches – St George's Bloomsbury and St George the Martyr (now St

Euterpe

Foundling Museum

The museum (entrance fee) tells the story of the Foundling Hospital, London's first home for abandoned children, founded and supported by three major figures in British history: philanthropist Sir Thomas Coram (1668-1751), artist William Hogarth (1697-1764) and composer George Frederic Handel (1685-1759). Coram founded the hospital after being appalled by the number of abandoned and orphaned children living on London's streets. The museum's collection charts the history of the Foundling Hospital from its foundation in 1739 to its closure in 1954. The hospital was also Britain's first unofficial public art gallery and exhibits paintings and sculptures donated by Hogarth, Thomas Gainsborough, Joshua Reynolds and others. (See https://foundlingmuseum.org.uk for information.)

George's Holborn). The gardens – where the first recorded case of 'body-snatching' took place in 1777 – are home to the terracotta statue of **Euterpe** , the Muse of Instrumental Music (1898), originally one of nine statues decorating the façade of the Apollo Inn in Tottenham Court Road. Exit the gardens via the footpath in the southwest corner to the **Foundling Museum** (see box), one of London's most poignant and intriguing collections. Outside the museum is William McMillan's (1963) superb bronze of **Sir Thomas Coram** , who

Walk 2

sits smiling with his hospital charter in his right hand.

Leaving the museum, follow the path to Brunswick Square and walk along the western edge to Grenville Street, turn right at the end and go left into Queen Anne's Walk to **Queen Square** **26**. Dating from around 1716, the square is a shady rectangle with a variety of trees, roses and bedding displays. At the north end of the square is a fine statue of **Queen Charlotte** **27** (erected in 1775, sculptor unknown), wife of George III; it was originally thought to have been of Queen Anne and the square was originally called Queen Anne's Square. On the corner of Cosmo Place is the **Queen's Larder** **28**, an intimate pub where, legend has it, Queen Charlotte stored food for the king when she was treating his illness in a nearby house on the square. In the middle of the square is a half torso and head sculpture of a **Mother and Child** **29** (2001) by Patricia Finch.

Francis Russell, 5th Duke of Bedford

Look out, too, for the sculpture of Sam the cat perched on a wall, a feline memorial to cat lover and champion of local causes, nurse Patricia Penn, unveiled in 1997.

At the southern end of the square is **St George's Holborn** **30** (aka St George the Martyr), built in 1703–06 by Arthur Tooley; it was once known as the sweeps' church, as parishioners provided Christmas dinner for 100 chimney sweeps' apprentices or 'climbing boys'. Walk along Cosmo Place (alongside the church) to Southampton Row and go left and then right into Bloomsbury Place and **Bloomsbury Square Garden** **31** (7.30am-dusk); one of London's earliest squares, it was developed by the 4th Earl of Southampton in the 1660s to complement his mansion. In the north of the square is Sir Richard Westmacott's (1816) bronze of **Charles James Fox** **32** (1749-1806), a Whig statesman and associate of the Dukes of Bedford.

On the south side of the square is another Westmacott statue, **Francis Russell, 5th Duke of Bedford** **33**, who was responsible for much of the development of central Bloomsbury. Erected in 1807, the statue depicts Russell as an agriculturalist with one hand on a plough, corn ears in the other and sheep at his feet, surveying

Mother and Child

the land he developed. From the north of the square continue along Bloomsbury Place into Great Russell Street, where on the right is the vast **British Museum** ㉞ (see box). Take a few minutes to admire the pediment (or tympanum) above the museum's south entrance (installed in 1851), which illustrates what 19th-century visitors would have found inside the museum.

Continue along Great Russell Street past the British Museum, cross over Bloomsbury Street and go left down Dyott Street to Congress House on the right, the HQ of the Trades Union Congress (TUC). Above the entrance is Bernard Meadows' bronze, **The Spirit of Brotherhood** ㉟,

Spirit of Brotherhood

representing the spirit of trade unionism with the strong helping the weak, while in the inner courtyard (reached via the main reception) is **Pietà** ㊱ by Jacob Epstein (1956), the striking TUC war memorial. Continue along Dyott Street, turn left on New Oxford Street and bear left into Bloomsbury Way; just past Museum Street on the left is **St George's Bloomsbury** ㊲, a Grade I listed English Baroque church. Built 1716-1731 and designed by Nicholas Hawksmoor (1661-1736), pupil and former assistant of Sir Christopher Wren, it's the architect's most idiosyncratic work. It combines Baroque splendour with classical references, topped by London's most eccentric spire, stepped like a pyramid and crowned by a statue of **George I** ㊳ in Roman dress posing as St George.

Continue along Bloomsbury Way and soon after Southampton Place, go right into **Sicilian Avenue** ㊴ (see box, page 34), one of Bloomsbury's most charming streets. If you fancy a drink or lunch, the **Holborn Whippet** 40 is a good choice. At the end of the avenue cross Southampton Row – note the former Kingsway Tram Tunnel in the middle of the road – and walk down to Catton Street. Set

---

British Museum

The British Museum is a London landmark and the country's most popular museum – attracting over 6 million visitors annually – and the fifth most-visited museum in the world. It provides an almost overwhelming smorgasbord of human history and culture stretching across centuries and continents, one that's best appreciated in small bites. The museum grew from the private collection of curiosities bequeathed to George II by physician and scientist, Sir Hans Sloane (1660-1753); established in 1753, it was the first national public museum in the world. It's still free to enter and enjoy. (See www.britishmuseum.org for information.)

Sicilian Avenue

Sicilian Avenue is so-named due to its authentic southern Italian feel, screened at both ends by Ionic columns and lined with Corinthian columns. Designed by Robert James Worley as a pedestrianised shopping street and completed in 1910, it was the inspiration of Herbrand Arthur Russell, 11th Duke of Bedford, who travelled to Sicily in the early 20th century. The avenue boasts beautiful architecture with ornate carved stone façades and walkways edged in Sicilian black and white marble, while down the centre are lamp standards and parasols.

into the corner on the first floor of the right-hand building – a former Baptist church – is a statue of **John Bunyan** ㊶ , author of *The Pilgrim's Progress*. Retrace your steps along Southampton Row and take Fisher Street to **Red Lion Square** ㊷ , laid out in 1684 by Nicholas Barbon. The square's gardens contain a

Margaret MacDonald memorial

number of statues, including Ian Walters' (1986) bronze of politician and anti-war activist **Fenner Brockway** ㊸ (1888-1988) and a memorial bust of philosopher **Bertrand Russell** ㊹ (1872-1970) by Marcelle Quinton (1980).

From the square head south along Drake Street, cross over High Holborn and take the Little Turnstile passage opposite to Gate Street which leads to **Lincoln's Inn Fields** ㊺ (7.30am to dusk). Designed by Inigo Jones in 1618, this is London's largest garden square (7.25 acres/2.9ha), which has been the site of jousting, notorious duels and the occasional public execution (Lord William Russell was beheaded – rather messily – here in 1688). To the right of the central north entrance is a lovely bronze memorial by Richard Reginald Goulden of **Margaret MacDonald** ㊻ (1896-1911), social reformer and wife of Prime Minister Ramsay MacDonald, who lived at number 3 Lincoln's Inn Fields. The fields also contain Nigel Boonham's bust of **John Hunter** ㊼ (1728-1793), the founder of scientific surgery, and the **Canadian Memorial** ㊽; a granite block adorned with a maple leaf in memory of the 85,000 Canadians who served in the Royal Canadian Air Force (its HQ was at number 20 Lincoln's Inn Fields) during the Second World War.

Opposite the entrance to the gardens is **Sir John Soane's Museum** ㊾ , one of London's most intriguing small museums, which showcases the famous architect's eclectic collection in his

Food & Drink

(7) Origin Coffee Roasters: A quick alternative to the Library's main eateries, Origin is a mecca for coffee connoisseurs (Mon-Thu 7am-6pm, Fri 7.30am-5.30pm, Sat 9am-4pm, Sun 10am-4pm, £).

(28) Queen's Larder: A traditional 18th-century pub on Queen Square with a nice terrace, offering good ales and pub grub (11.30am-11pm, Sat noon-11pm, Sun noon-10.30pm, £).

(40) Holborn Whippet: A fine pub on Sicilian Avenue serving a wide choice of craft beers and authentic pizzas (Mon-Sat, noon-11pm, closed Sun, £).

passageway just past the Cittie of Yorke pub – leading to **Gray's Inn (51)** – one of the four Inns of Court for barristers – where, in the South Square, is Frederick William Pomeroy's (1912) splendid statue of **Sir Francis Bacon (52)** (1561-1626). Bacon was admitted to the Inn in 1576 and called to the Bar in 1582; he was elected Treasurer in 1608 and held the position until 1617, when he was appointed Lord High Chancellor under James I.

From the square, retrace your steps to High Holborn and turn left towards Chancery Lane tube station, and the end of the walk.

Sir Francis Bacon

former home (www.soane.org); note the distinctive façade in white Norfolk brick and the figures at the second-floor level. In the northeast corner of the square, adjacent to Newman's Row, is **Camdonian (50)**, a work in sheet steel sprayed in bronze by Barry Flanagan (1980). From here, turn left along Newman's Row to Great Turnstile, a passage leading to High Holborn, where you cross over and go right. Around 50m further on turn left along the

1. Royal Tank Regiment
2. Brigade of Gurkhas
3. Earth and Water
4. 8th Duke of Devonshire
5. Banqueting House
6. The Lord Moon of the Mall
7. Field Marshal Earl Haig
8. Women of World War II Memorial
9. Viscounts Slim, Alanbrooke & Montgomery
10. Cenotaph
11. Parliament Square Garden
12. Sir Winston Churchill
13. David Lloyd George
14. Jan Christiaan Smuts
15. Viscount Palmerston
16. 14th Earl of Derby
17. Benjamin Disraeli
18. Sir Robert Peel
19. Mahatma Gandhi

Charing Cross Station

NORTHUMBERLAN

WHITEHALL
WHITEHALL
WHITEHALL

Horse Guards Parade

DOWNING ST

HORSE GUA

RICHMO

KING CHARLES STREET

St James's Park

GREAT GEORGE ST

BRID

See enlarged detail

BIRDCAGE WALK

BRID

PETTY FRANCE

TOTHILL STREET

VICTORIA STREET

ABINGDON ST

MILLBANK

END

St James's Park tube

BROADWAY

ST ANN'S ST

GREAT PETER STREET

MARSHAM STREET

GREAT GEORGE ST

PARLIAMENT SQUARE

PARLIAMENT SQUARE

Places of Interest   Food & Drink

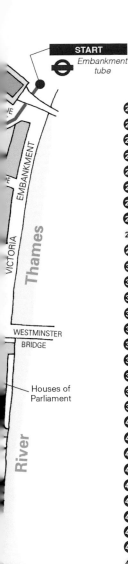

WALK 3

Whitehall to
St James's

Walk 3

> **Distance:** 2¾ miles (4½ km)
> **Terrain:** easy
> **Duration:** 2 hours
> **Start:** Embankment tube
> **End:** St James's Park tube
> **Postcode:** WC2N 6NS

WHITEHALL TO ST JAMES'S

Statesmen, politicians, monarchs and military men – these are among the many kinds of VIP commemorated by statues and monuments on this stroll through the political heartland of London. We begin on Whitehall, named after the Palace of Whitehall, the principal residence of English monarchs from 1530 (Henry VIII) until 1698 (William III). The palace was destroyed by fire in 1698 – only Inigo Jones' 1662 Banqueting House survived – but Whitehall is still at the centre of British government, lined with numerous departments and ministries.

From Whitehall we continue via Parliament Street, to Parliament Square, where many eminent British and foreign statesmen are honoured, including Winston Churchill, Mahatma Gandhi, Abraham Lincoln and Nelson Mandela. Here, in the heart of Westminster – home to the Palace of Westminster (aka the Houses of Parliament) and Westminster Abbey, where England's monarchs have been crowned since 1066 – you'll find one of the highest concentrations of historic landmarks in London.

We then head south to Victoria Tower Gardens and west to the affluent district of St James's – ironically named after a 12th-century leper hospital – to tour more historic streets and monuments. After skirting St James's Park and visiting the Guards Museum we end at St James's Park tube station, beneath the Art Deco majesty of the former London Underground HQ.

Start Walking…

Exit Embankment tube station and turn right, passing under Hungerford and Golden Jubilee Bridges to go right onto Northumberland Avenue. Turn left on Whitehall Place and left again to Whitehall Court. On the right-hand corner is Vivien Mallock's memorial to the **Royal Tank Regiment** ❶ (RTR), which depicts the five-man crew of a Second World War-era Comet tank; unveiled in 2000, it's an enlarged version of a maquette by George Henry Paulin on view in the Tank Regiment Museum in Bovington, Dorset. Mallock's husband had been an officer in the RTR in the '60s. At the end of Whitehall Court turn right into Horse Guards Avenue, where on the corner is Philip Jackson's memorial to the **Brigade of Gurkhas** ❷ , which is modelled on a 1924 statue by Richard Reginald Goulden located in the Foreign Office. The first memorial to the Gurkhas in the UK, the inscription is taken from a quotation by Sir Ralph Turner (1888-1983), an English Indian languages philologist: 'Bravest of the brave, most generous of the generous, never had a country more faithful friends than you'.

Opposite the Gurkha statue, flanking the entrance to the Ministry of Defence, are two huge sculptures by Charles Wheeler (1949) – a pair of reclining giantesses – symbolising **Earth and Water** ❸ , each carved from 40 tonnes of Portland stone. They were supposed to be

The Gurkhas

The name 'Gurkha' comes from the Gorkha Kingdom of Nepal, forerunner of modern Nepal. Gurkhas have been part of the British Army for over 200 years since the invasion of Nepal in 1814 when, after suffering heavy casualties, the British East India Company wisely signed a peace deal that allowed it to recruit from the ranks of its former enemy. Following the partition of India in 1947, an agreement between Nepal, India and Britain led to four Gurkha regiments transferring to the British Army, eventually becoming the Gurkha Brigade. Gurkhas are closely associated with the kukri (or khukuri), a forward-curving 18-inch Nepalese knife, and have a well-earned reputation for fearless military prowess.

complemented by similar figures representing Air and Fire, but the Treasury baulked at the cost and they were never completed. Turn right on Horse Guards Avenue from the Gurkha statue where, at the end – opposite the Horse

Earth & Water

Guards building – is Herbert Hampton's (1911) bronze of statesman Spencer Compton Cavendish, **8th Duke of Devonshire** ❹ (1833-1908). Just past the statue, on the corner of Whitehall above the ground floor entrance to **Banqueting House** ❺, is an anonymous bust of Charles I. It recalls the king's execution in 1649 outside the building. If you fancy a coffee or breakfast, there isn't much choice in the immediate vicinity, but if you

Banqueting House

The Cenotaph

Designed by Sir Edwin Lutyens, the Portland stone Cenotaph – the word means a monument to someone buried elsewhere, in particular those killed in warfare – was unveiled on Armistice Day in 1920. An annual Service of Remembrance is held at the site on Remembrance Sunday, the closest Sunday to 11th November (Armistice Day) each year. Lutyens' cenotaph design has been reproduced elsewhere in the UK and in other countries, including Australia, Canada, New Zealand and Hong Kong. The monument – 35ft (11m) tall and weighing 120 tonnes – has no decoration other than a carved wreath on each end and a smaller wreath at the top, with the words 'The Glorious Dead' inscribed below the wreaths on each end. The Cenotaph is adorned on each side by flags of the United Kingdom.

---

go right along Whitehall there are a number of options, including **The Lord Moon of the Mall** ❻, a grand Wetherspoon pub around 150m along on the left (open from 8am).

Retrace your steps to Banqueting House, where a short distance along (in the middle of the road) is Alfred Frank Hardiman's equestrian bronze statue of a hatless (heaven forbid!) **Field Marshal Earl Haig** ❼, Commander-in-Chief of the British Armies in France 1915-1918. Some 100m further on (opposite the Cabinet Office) is the imposing, if somewhat bland, **Women of World War II Memorial** ❽, a 2005 bronze sculpture by John William Mills. The abstract sculpture is a long cuboid adorned with hanging female garments, both military and civilian, symbolising the contribution of women to Britain's victory in the Second World War.

Opposite the memorial, in front of the Ministry of Defence, is a trio of Field Marshals: from north to south, **Viscounts Slim, Alanbrooke and Montgomery** ❾. Field Marshals Slim (1891-1970) and Alanbrooke (1883-

1963) are both by Ivor Roberts-Jones, unveiled in 1990 and 1993 respectively, while Field Marshal Montgomery (1887-1976) of Alamein is a 1980 bronze by Oscar Nemon. A short distance along, just past the entrance to Downing Street, is the Grade I listed **Cenotaph** ⑩ (see box opposite), Britain's most famous war memorial.

As Whitehall becomes Parliament Street, you pass the Treasury building on the right and cross Bridge Street to enter **Parliament Square Garden** ⑪, the site of a wealth of fine statues, mainly politicians and statesmen, British and foreign. The first one you see, in the northeast corner, is Ivor Roberts-Jones' vast bronze of **Sir Winston Churchill** ⑫ (1874-1965), unveiled in 1973. The bronze stands 12ft (3.6m) on an 8ft (2.4m) pedestal and perfectly captures the character of one of Britain's greatest statesmen. Going anti-clockwise, the next statue is Glynn Williams' 2007 bronze of **David Lloyd George** ⑬ (1863-1945) – it isn't considered to be a very characterful representation of the former PM who served 1916-1922 – flanked by Sir Jacob Epstein's (1956) bronze of **Jan Christiaan Smuts** ⑭ (1870-1950), the 2nd Prime Minister of South Africa (1919-1924 and again 1939-1948),

Sir Winston Churchill

portrayed in a Field Marshal's uniform on a pedestal of South African granite. A little further along is Thomas Woolner's 1876 statue of **Viscount Palmerston** ⑮ (1784-1865), who served twice as PM (1855-1858, 1859-1865) and in various other Cabinet posts.

Along the western edge of the square (starting in the northwest corner) is Edward Smith-Stanley, **14th Earl of Derby** ⑯ (1799-1869) by Matthew Noble; three times Prime Minister (1852, 1858-59, 1866-68), Smith-Stanley is portrayed wearing his robes as Chancellor of Oxford University. He's followed by Mario Raggi's bronze of **Benjamin Disraeli** ⑰ (1804-1881), 1st Earl of Beaconsfield; a distinguished and popular Prime Minister (1868, 1874-1880), Disraeli was born into a Jewish family but was baptised as a Christian at the age of 12. Next along is **Sir Robert Peel** ⑱ (1788-1850) by Matthew Noble, unveiled in 1877. Peel was Prime Minister from 1834-1835 and 1841-1846 and is credited with creating the modern police service (the 'Peelers'). In front of Peel is a wonderful portrayal of **Mahatma Gandhi** ⑲ (1869-1948) by Philip Jackson (2015). The leader of the Indian independence movement and unofficial 'father of the Indian nation', Gandhi was assassinated in 1948, less than six months after

Millicent Fawcett

India gained independence from Britain.

A little way along from Ghandi in the southwest corner is Ian Walters' bronze of **Nelson Mandela** ㉒ (1918-2013), President of South Africa 1994-1999 and one of the world's most revered statesmen. The statue was unveiled in 2007 by Prime Minister Gordon Brown in the presence of Mandela. In 2018, Gillian Wearing's bronze of **Millicent Fawcett** ㉑ (1847-1929) was unveiled in the square, the first statue of a woman to be erected there. British feminist, intellectual, political leader, and writer, Fawcett is primarily known

for her work as a campaigner for women to have the vote and is depicted holding a banner reading: 'Courage calls to courage everywhere'.

To the west of Parliament Square, on a separate strip of grass, is a bronze of US President **Abraham Lincoln** ㉒ (1809-1865), a replica of a statue by Augustus Saint-Gaudens in Lincoln Park, Chicago. North of Lincoln, at the junction with Great George Street, is Sir Richard Westmacott's (1832) statue of **George Canning** ㉓ (1770-1827), who served in various Cabinet positions (notably as Foreign Secretary) and was briefly Prime Minister in 1827, when he died in office after just 119 days (the shortest tenure of any PM). In the southwest corner of the square (almost opposite Lincoln) is the **Supreme Court** ㉔ (see box), housed in the splendid Gothic extravaganza that is Middlesex Guildhall (Grade II* listed).

Along Broad Sanctuary, opposite the west entrance of **Westminster Abbey** ㉕ , is Sir George Gilbert Scott's imposing **Crimea & Indian Mutiny Memorial** ㉖ , aka the Westminster Scholars War Memorial, a tall marble and stone column erected in 1861. It's in memory of the former pupils of Westminster School who died in the Crimean War (1854-56) and the Indian Mutiny (1857-58). Its fine detail includes statues of Edward the Confessor, Henry III, Elizabeth I and Queen Victoria by John Birnie Philip, topped by

Supreme Court

Designed by the Scottish architect James S. Gibson and constructed in 1912-13 – in what architectural expert Nikolaus Pevsner termed 'Art Nouveau Gothic' – the Supreme Court is decorated with fantastical medieval-looking gargoyles and other architectural sculptures by Henry Charles Fehr. Most impressive of all is the relief frieze above and to the sides of the entrance.

Whitehall to St James's

St Margaret's Church

Food & Drink

6 **The Lord Moon of the Mall:** Grand Wetherspoon pub on Whitehall which does coffee and breakfast, etc. (8am-11pm/midnight, £).

28 **Cellarium Café & Terrace:** Westminster Abbey's café is set in the monks' original larder; licensed, it serves imaginative salads and tasty mains (Mon-Fri, 8am-6pm, Sat 9am-5pm, Sun 10am-4pm, £).

49 **The Feathers:** If you fancy a drink (or lunch) at the end of the walk, this pub opposite St James's tube station is a good pit stop (020-7227 0921, 11am-11pm, £).

Century Fund – or the 'Million Guinea Fund' as it became known – which raised one million guineas from one million Methodists. The hall has some particularly beautiful spandrels by Henry Poole, depicting angels. If you're in need of refreshment, the **Cellarium Café & Terrace 28** in Westminster Abbey (free access) is an atmospheric spot, set in the monks' original larder. It's accessed via the Sanctuary (just behind the Crimea memorial) in

St George slaying the dragon by John Richard Clayton.

Opposite the statue on Storey's Gate is the magnificent **Central Hall Westminster 27**, aka Methodist Central Hall, designed by Edwin Alfred Rickards in Viennese Baroque style with Romanesque decoration. The hall was built in 1905-11 to mark the centenary of the death of John Wesley (founder of Methodism) in 1791 and was funded by the Wesleyan Methodist Twentieth

St Margaret's Church

Standing between Westminster Abbey and the Houses of Parliament, St Margaret's is believed to have been built in the latter part of the 11th century. The church is dedicated to the little-known St Margaret of Antioch, one of the most popular saints among the laity in medieval England. St Margaret's became the parish church of the Palace of Westminster in 1614, when Puritans – unhappy with the highly liturgical Abbey – chose to hold Parliamentary services there. This practice continues to this day and has led St Margaret's to be dubbed 'the parish church of the House of Commons'.

the northeast corner of Dean's Yard.

Return to Parliament Square past **St Margaret's Church** ㉙ (see box, page 43) and turn right down St Margaret Street, where there's a controversial statue of **Oliver Cromwell** ㉚ by Hamo Thorneycroft (1899), depicting the Lord Protector holding a sword and a bible, with a lion on the base. The statue has long divided opinion due to Cromwell's opposition to the British monarchy and his role in the conquest of Ireland, where he's accused of war crimes, religious persecution and the ethnic cleansing of Catholics. Opposite Cromwell is, ironically, a bust of **Charles I** ㉛ – the king Cromwell had beheaded – mounted in a niche in the east wall of St Margaret's Church. It's thought to date from around 1800 (sculptor unknown) and was installed here in 1956.

Continuing along St Margaret Street into Abingdon Street, on the right you'll see William Reid Dick's (1947) statue of **George V** ㉜, with the king depicted in Field Marshal's uniform and

Knife Edge Two Piece 1962-65

Garter robes. Almost opposite in Old Palace Yard is Baron Carlo Marochetti's (1856) splendid equestrian statue of **Richard I** ㉝ (1157-1199), aka Richard the Lionheart, the (mostly absent) Crusader king who ruled from 1189 until his death and is buried in Fontevraud Abbey in Anjou, France. Look back across the road to see the 16 gilt weather vanes – bearing various Tudor emblems, such as the portcullis, falcon and greyhound – on the roof of the Chapel of Henry VII at the eastern end of Westminster Abbey. They were donated by the Royal Institution of Chartered Surveyors (RICS) to commemorate the centenary of its charter in 1981. Just past the Abbey is the 14th-century Jewel Tower and beyond it Abingdon Street Gardens, with Henry Moore's abstract bronze **Knife Edge Two Piece 1962-65** ㉞ in the middle – a rare exception to the wealth of figurative statuary on this walk. Just over Millbank is **Victoria Tower Gardens** ㉟ (open 5am-10pm).

Enter the gardens via the gate in the northwest corner, where immediately opposite the entrance is Arthur George Walker's fine

Richard I

statue of suffragette leader
Emmeline Pankhurst 36 (1858-
1928), who endured many spells
of imprisonment to win women
the right to vote. It was erected
just two years after her death in
1928, a month before all women
aged 21 or over could finally
vote in elections. Follow the
path around to the right, where
on the left is a cast of Auguste
Rodin's magnificent bronze,
The Burghers of Calais 37 ,
completed in 1889 and installed
here in 1915. It commemorates
a pivotal moment in 1347 during
the Hundred Years' War, when the
French port of Calais was under
siege by the English and six civic
notables gave themselves up in
an act of self-sacrifice to save their
fellow townspeople (they were
spared by Edward III). At the far
end of the garden is the glorious
Buxton Memorial Fountain 38
(see box).

The Burghers of Calais

Buxton Memorial Fountain

This grand neo-
Gothic confection
commemorates
the abolition of
slavery in the British
Empire in 1834.
Commissioned by
Charles Buxton MP
– who campaigned
against slavery
in Parliament –
and designed by
Samuel Sanders Teulon in 1865 (by
coincidence, the same year that the
US passed the 13th Amendment
outlawing slavery), it originally stood
in Parliament Square but has been
located here since 1957. Additional
figures by Thomas Earp have been
lost.

Leave the gardens opposite
the fountain to Millbank and cross
over to Dean Stanley Street and
St John's, Smith Square 39 .
Designed by Thomas Archer
(1668-1743) and completed in
1728, St John's is regarded as a
masterpiece of English Baroque
architecture (Grade I listed). It
was gutted by fire during the Blitz,
leaving only a shell for over 20
years, until being resurrected in
the '60s as a concert hall; today,
it's one of London's finest concert
halls.

From the square take Dean
Trench Street heading west and
turn right on Tufton Street and
then left down Bennett's Yard to
Marsham Street. Head right past
the Emmanuel Centre – home to
the Emmanuel Evangelical Church
– and go left along Great Peter
Street (named for the Abbey of St
Peter aka Westminster Abbey) and
right along St Ann's Street, past
St Matthew's Westminster (the
work of Sir George Gilbert Scott).
After around 100m take the first
left on Old Pye Street – this area
was known as the Devil's Acre in

the 19th century, when it was one of the worst slums in London. Go right at the end to Strutton Ground and then left on Victoria Street.

Guards Chapel

Adjacent to the Guards Museum is the Guards Chapel. In 1944 the original chapel (built in 1838) was totally destroyed by a V1 flying bomb during the morning service, which claimed 121 lives and injured 140. It was rebuilt in the '60s in a modern style. Outside the west end of the chapel stands James Butler's outstanding 1985 bronze of Field Marshal **Earl Alexander of Tunis** ㊺ (1891-1969), who served with distinction in both World Wars and oversaw the evacuation from Dunkirk in 1940.

Opposite, on the corner with Broadway, are Christchurch Gardens, where you find Glynn Williams' memorial to **Henry Purcell** ㊵

Henry Purcell memorial

(1659-1695), unveiled by Princess Margaret in 1995 on the tercentenary of his death. Also known as the 'Flowering of the English Baroque', it's an odd statue, consisting of a large figurative head surmounted by a 'headdress' of flowers. In the northwest corner of the gardens is Edwin Russell's bronze **Suffragette Memorial** ㊶ , unveiled on 14th July 1970 (Emmeline Pankhurst's birthday) and commissioned by the Suffragette Fellowship. In the form of a scroll, it's inscribed: 'To commemorate the courage and perseverance of all those men and women who in the long struggle for votes for women selflessly braved derision, opposition and ostracism, many enduring physical violence and suffering'.

Go north on Broadway, turn right at the end along Tothill Street and then left into Dartmouth Street. Take the first left on Queen Anne's Gate, where on the left against the wall of number 15 is a Portland stone statue of **Queen Anne** ㊷ (1665-1714), dating from around 1705 (sculptor unknown). Continue along Queen Anne's Gate and as the road swings left, take the path on the right to Birdcage Walk. Opposite is the marble **Boy Statue** ㊸ , designed by Charles Henry Mabey (1863), set on a plinth. Originally a drinking fountain, the water came from the mouths of four fish and collected in shell-shaped basins. Around 100m further along, in Wellington Barracks, is the **Guards Museum** ㊹ , which traces the history of the five regiments of Foot Guards – Grenadier, Coldstream, Scots, Irish and Welsh Guards – which, together with the two regiments of Household Cavalry (the Life Guards and the Blues and Royals), comprise Her Majesty's Household Division (see www. theguardsmuseum.com).

Take the path alongside the museum to Petty France, turn left and go across the roundabout to Broadway, where **55 Broadway** ㊻

Whitehall to St James's

55 Broadway

Also known as the London Underground Headquarters, 55 Broadway is a dramatic Art Deco building (Grade I listed) straddling St James's Park tube station. Designed by Charles Holden and built in 1927-1929, it was considered an architectural masterpiece and Holden was awarded the RIBA London Architecture Medal for it in 1931. The ground floor is traversed by three Travertine marble-clad and paved public arcades, which retain their ornamental ventilation grilles in a geometric design. Other features include wall clocks set into a low-relief sunburst in Travertine marble, polygonal marble-clad columns and coffered ceilings.

sculptors of the day, who included Eric Aumonier, Alfred Gerrard, Eric Gill (who did three sculptures), Henry Moore, Samuel Rabinovitch and Allan Wyon.

This marks the end of the walk, which conveniently coincides with St James's Park tube station. If you fancy a drink or a bite to eat, opposite is Nicholson's traditional Victorian pub, **The Feathers** **49**, serving real ales and quality pub grub.

55 Broadway

(see box) – the old London Transport HQ – displays ten sculptures. Halfway along the north and east façades are a matched pair of graphic naked figures, **Day** and **Night** **47**, by Jacob Epstein. The sculptures created public outrage on their unveiling, which led to Epstein agreeing to remove 1½ inches from the penis (ouch!) of the smaller figure (Day) and, eventually, the furore died down. On each elevation, the pediment above the sixth floor is decorated with a relief representing **The Four Winds** **48**, each sculpture being repeated twice, making a total of eight. The eight reliefs were carved by leading avant-garde

Day & Night

The Four Winds

INNER CIRCLE

CHESTER ROAD

BROAD WALK

Regent's Park

OUTER CIRCLE

MARYLEBONE ROAD

PARK CRES

CORNWALL TERR

ALLSOP PL

BAKER STREET

PORTLAND PL

END
Baker
Street tube

CAVENDISH

SQUARE

OXF

1. William Pitt the Younger
2. Winged Figure
3. Lord George Bentinck
4. Madonna and Child
5. All Souls Church
6. John Nash
7. BBC Broadcasting House
8. Prospero and Ariel
9. Breathing
10. Quintin & Alice Hogg
11. Sir George White
12. General Sikorski
13. Royal Institute of British Architects
14. Bistro at 66

Places of Interest ○ Food & Drink

WALK 4

START
Oxford Circus tube

D STREET

HANOVER ST

Oxford Circus to Marylebone

Walk 4

Distance: 3¾ miles (6 km)
Terrain: easy
Duration: 2-3 hours
Start: Oxford Circus tube
End: Baker Street tube
Postcode: W1B 3AG

This walk commences at the epicentre of West End retail culture, Oxford Circus, where Oxford Street and Regent Street intersect. Oxford Street was originally a Roman road and is now Europe's busiest shopping street, with around 300 shops and over half a million visitors every day. From Oxford Circus we visit Hanover Square and Cavendish Square Gardens, before heading north along Portland Place – home to the BBC's Broadcasting House. The street was laid out by Robert and James Adam in the 18th century for the Duke of Portland, and still contains some of their handsome Georgian terraced houses, as well as many fine memorials.

At the northern end of Portland Place is the affluent district of Marylebone, which gets its name from a church dedicated to St Mary, now represented by St Marylebone Parish Church. Across Marylebone Road is Regent's Park, the largest of central London's five royal parks at 410 acres (166ha), and a repository of some fine public art. The English Garden (Avenue Gardens), north of Portland Place (via Park Square), is also the venue for some excellent sculpture exhibitions, including the outdoor Frieze Sculpture Park. From here, we head west to the Inner Circle, a treasure house of horticulture and statuary; not least Queen Mary's Rose Gardens and the 'secret' St John's Lodge Garden.

We finish at Baker Street tube station, where (appropriately) there's a statue of the fictional detective Sherlock Holmes who 'lived' at 221B Baker Street.

Oxford Circus

OXFORD CIRCUS TO MARYLEBONE

Oxford Circus to Marylebone

Start Walking…

Leave Oxford Circus tube station, head south along the right-hand side of Regent Street, and take the second right into Hanover Street and Hanover Square to see Sir Francis Chantrey's statue of **William Pitt the Younger** ❶. Pitt (1759-1806) was the UK's youngest Prime Minister – he took office in 1783 at the tender age of 24 and served until 1801 – who also served a second term in 1804-6, dying in office aged

just 46. He's known as 'the Younger' to distinguish him from his father, William Pitt the Elder (1708-1778), who was Prime Minister 1766-68. The statue, at the south end of Hanover Square, was unveiled in 1831 and survived an attempt by Reform Bill agitators to pull it down the same day. From the square take Harewood Place north, crossing Oxford Street to Holles Street where, on the side of the John Lewis building, is Barbara Hepworth's **Winged Figure** ❷ (Grade II* listed). Installed in 1963, the work is 19ft (5.8m) in height – made of aluminium and stainless steel – and resembles a boat's hull, with two wide asymmetric wing-like blades rising from a small plinth, curving towards each other and linked by a series of radial rods.

Continue up Holles Street to Cavendish Square Gardens, laid out in 1717 by John Prince for the 2nd Earl of Oxford and named after the Earl's wife Henrietta Cavendish-Holles. On the south side of the square is Thomas Campbell's fine bronze of **Lord George Bentinck** ❸ (1802-1848), a wealthy, though not very distinguished, late 19th-century Conservative MP; his most notable act was leading the opposition to the repeal of the Corn Laws. North of the square is Jacob Epstein's 1953 work, **Madonna and Child** ❹, a large lead sculpture installed on a bridge over the entrance to Dean's Mews. Forming part of the rebuilt Convent of the Holy Child Jesus after damage during the Second

Madonna & Child

Walk 4

World War, it's one of Epstein's most celebrated works. From Dean's Mews head east along Cavendish Place and turn left on Langham Place, passing The Langham (hotel) on the left and **All Souls Church** **⑤** on the right. An evangelical Anglican church, All Souls was designed

Prospero and Ariel

Broadcasting House

Nash **⑥** (1752-1835) by Cecil Thomas.

Next to All Souls is **BBC Broadcasting House** **⑦** (see box, page 51), headquarters of the BBC. It's decorated with works by the controversial sculptor, Eric Gill, including the statues of **Prospero and Ariel** **⑧** which hover over the main entrance. These characters (from Shakespeare's *The Tempest*) were deemed appropriate for the building because Prospero was a magician and Ariel was a spirit of the air (radio waves, of course, travel in air). True to his nature, Gill carved a girl's face into Prospero's backside and gave Ariel rather large genitals, which he later had to reduce in size! He also insisted on working on the statues wearing a monk's habit with nothing on underneath.

To the right of the original building is the new East Wing of Broadcasting House, completed in 2005 and later named

in Regency style by John Nash (the only Nash church in London) and consecrated in 1824. The church has a striking circular spired vestibule, where to the right of the entrance, is a bust of **John**

Breathing

after much-loved DJ John Peel (1939-2004). Rising from the top floor is **Breathing** ❾ , a sculpture by Catalan artist Jaume Plensa, a memorial to news reporters and crew, both BBC and non-BBC, who have died on assignments. Consisting of a 33ft (10m) high inverted glass spire, the sculpture is lit during the hours of darkness and, in tandem with the 10pm news bulletin, a fine beam of light is projected 3,000ft (900m) into the night sky.

Quintin & Alice Hogg memorial

RIBA HQ Sculptures

The sculpted figures on the RIBA building's façade depict the creative forces of architecture. The central figure above the entrance – depicting Architectural Aspiration – is by Edward Bainbridge Copnall, while the figures on the columns – the spirits of man and woman – are by James Woodford. Along the Weymouth Street elevation are five more relief figures by Copnall: a painter, sculptor, architect (Sir Christopher Wren), engineer and 'working man'. Also of note are Woodford's massive cast bronze doors, each weighing 1½ tonnes. The deep relief design depicts the Thames and some of London's landmarks, including the Guildhall and the Houses of Parliament (left-hand door), and St Paul's and Horse Guards (right-hand door). The three children on the right-hand door are those of the building's architect, George Grey Wornum. The bronze railing designs above the door and the figure of Mercury on the concealed letter box (at the base of the right-hand column) are by Seton White.

From Broadcasting House walk north along Portland Place. In the centre of the road is George Frampton's (1906) memorial to philanthropists **Quintin & Alice Hogg** ❿ (1845-1903 and 1845-1918 respectively). The bronze, on a Portland stone plinth, depicts Quintin reading to two boys. Further along the street, just before Weymouth Street, is John Tweed's impressive equestrian statue of Field Marshal **Sir George White** ⓫ (1835-1912), unveiled in 1922. White had a distinguished army career serving in India and Afghanistan, where his bravery won him the Victoria Cross. He also served in Burma, Sudan and Natal, where he was the hero of the Siege of Ladysmith during the Boer War. On the other side of Weymouth Street is Faith Winter's fine statue of **General Sikorski** ⓬ (1881-1943). Wladyslaw Sikorski was Commander-in-Chief of the Polish Armed Forces from 1939 to 1943, when he was killed in a plane crash in Gibraltar.

To the right of the general, on the corner of Weymouth Street, is the HQ of the **Royal Institute of British Architects/RIBA** ⓭ (see box), designed by George Grey

Wornum and opened in 1934 by George V. Faced in Portland stone with rich applied decoration and sculpture, it's a prime example of '30s Art Deco architecture. The interior is also striking, and has the bonus of an excellent café/restaurant, **Bistro at 66 ⑭**.

Mother and Child

Around 200m further on, near the end of Portland Place, is Thomas Brock's (1922) characterful memorial to **Sir Joseph Lister ⑮** (1827-1912). It comprises a bust of Lister – pioneer of antiseptic surgery – mounted on a high pedestal with a life-size woman and boy at the front. At the end of Portland Place cross over Park Crescent, where Sebastian Gahagan's (1820s) superb statue of **Prince Edward, Duke of Kent ⑯** (1767-1820) is located in the private garden behind the railings. At the eastern end of the crescent, around the corner on Marylebone Road (actually number 1 Park Crescent), is American Jacques Lipchitz's bust of **President John F. Kennedy ⑰** (1917-1963), mounted on a pedestal of polished black granite. It was unveiled in 1965 by his brother Robert,

three years before he, too, was assassinated.

Just past the statue turn right and make a short detour down Great Portland Street to the Portland Hospital for Women and Children, around 100m along on the right. It's the maternity hospital of choice for royals and celebrities, where in a niche in the front wall is David Norris' (1983) graceful sculpture **Mother and Child ⑱**, which portrays a child balanced on its mother's arm. Retrace your steps to Marylebone Road,

Food & Drink

⑭ Bistro at 66: A splendid café/restaurant in the RIBA building offering superb food in an Art Deco dining room (020-7307 3744, Mon-Fri 10am-3.30pm, £-££).

㉘ The Regent's Bar & Kitchen: The original '60s park café has been refurbished and offers drinks, lunch and supper in lush garden surroundings (8am to 8pm, 6pm in winter, £).

㉞ The Volunteer: A cosy Victorian pub on Baker Street, serving excellent ales and wholesome pub grub (10am-midnight, Sunday noon-midnight, £).

Queen Mary's Rose Gardens

Named after the wife of George V, the gardens were laid out in 1932 and contain London's largest and best formal rose collection. They're a honeypot for garden lovers (and bees) in spring and summer, when thousands of plants are in bloom. As well as the glorious roses, the delightful gardens feature the national collection of delphiniums and some 9,000 begonias, laid out in landscaped beds surrounded by a ring of pillars covered in climbers and ramblers.

cross over and go left to Park Square East, and walk along the edge of Park Square (private) to the Outer Circle and **Regent's Park** ⑲ (5am-dusk). Enter the park via the Broad Walk through the sumptuous Avenue Gardens, where in the centre stands a large circular stone bowl supported by four winged stone lions, known as the **Griffin Tazza** ⑳ aka the Lion Vase. It was designed by Austin and Seely and installed by landscape architect William Andrews Nesfield in 1863.

Continue along the Broad Walk to Chester Road, and turn left to the **Inner Circle** ㉑. Take the first left and go through **Queen Mary's Rose Gardens** ㉒ (see box) and continue, with the lake on your right, to the Japanese Garden Island. Cross over to the island on the wooden bow bridge and follow the path round to the right. Here there's an **Eagle Sculpture** ㉓,

presented to the Royal Parks in 1974, believed to be of Japanese origin (hence its location). On the other side of the island there's a stunning waterfall. Return to the main path and continue west where, on the left, is the main entrance to the Inner Circle distinguished by the grand gilded, semi-circular **Jubilee Gates** ㉔, donated by Sigismund Goetze (1866-1939) – an artist and art patron with a particular passion for Regent's Park – and installed to mark the Silver Jubilee of George V and the official opening of the gardens in 1935.

Turn right onto the central path and walk to the top of the Inner Circle to see the beautiful **Triton Fountain** ㉕, designed by William McMillan in 1936. The fountain,

Triton Fountain

depicting a sea god or triton blowing on a conch shell with mermaids at his feet, was donated in memory of Sigismund Goetze by his wife Constance, though not installed until 1950, a decade after his death. Nearby are two works by Albert Hemstock Hodge: **The Lost Bow & The Mighty Hunter** ㉖. The Lost Bow depicts a helmeted cherub seated on a vulture – another Goetze donation, along with the Boy and Frog statue (see below) – while The Mighty

Hunter shows a cherub holding a goose, donated by Duncan Campbell. Continue round the Inner Circle in an anti-clockwise direction, passing the Open Air Theatre, a permanent venue opened in 1932, with a three- to four-month summer season. In a pond near the western entrance to the gardens is Sir William Reid Dick's (1936) **Boy and Frog Statue** 27, a bronze sculpture on a pedestal of Finnish granite. Just inside the garden entrance is the **Regent's Bar & Kitchen** 28 – the perfect spot for coffee or lunch.

Hylas & the Nymph

Leave the gardens here and go right (or clockwise) around the Inner Circle for around 400m, past a path to the left leading to the Long Bridge and the Boating Lake. A little further on, in the northeast of the Inner Circle, there's a 'hidden' path (it's easy to miss) on the left with an arched pergola that leads to the enchanting 'secret' **St John's Lodge Garden** 29 (see box opposite). The handsome lodge was the first house built in Regent's Park in 1817-19, designed by John Raffield for Charles Augustus Tulk MP. It was one of over 50 grand villas envisaged by John Nash in his plan to transform the park and surrounding area in the 1800s, although only eight were built. In front of the lodge are six stone piers topped by boys holding armorial shields, which were probably installed for the Marquess of Bute; three were designed by Sir William Goscombe John in 1894 and one by Harold Youngman in 1938 (the remaining two are undated).

Sir John's Lodge Garden contains a number of statues, including Henry Pegram's bronze centrepiece, **Hylas and the Nymph** 30, mounted on a stone pedestal set in a stone-rimmed pond. It depicts a boy with a sensual mermaid seizing his legs and attempting to pull him to his doom; in Greek mythology, Hylas was one of the Argonauts who accompanied Jason on the quest for the Golden Fleece. During the journey, Hylas was kidnapped by the nymph of spring and never seen again. Off to one side is **The Goatherd's Daughter** 31, aka The Shepherdess, by Charles Leonard Hartwell; it's a bronze depicting a semi-draped shepherdess holding a young goat. Erected in 1932 by the National Council for Animal Welfare in honour of its founders Harold and Gertrude Baillie Weaver, it bears the inscription: 'To all the Protectors of the

Defenceless'. Located in the front right section of the garden is Wuts Safardiar's (ca. 2000) beautiful bronze, **The Awakening** 32, dedicated 'In fond memory of Anne Lydia Evans (1929-1999) who shared the secret of this garden'. Anne was a Marylebone GP who worked on the Medical Campaign for the Care of Victims of Torture and is described as compassionate and fair, with a deep social conscience'.

Leave the garden, retrace your steps to the Regent's Bar & Kitchen and take the path opposite leading past the **Bandstand** 33. In 1982, the band of the Royal Green Jackets was the target of an IRA terrorist bomb here, which left seven soldiers dead and 24 injured. A small plaque on the bandstand commemorates the victims of the attack. Follow the path along the edge of the lake to Clarence Gate and Bridge, where you exit the park. Cross over to the Outer Circle and go down Baker Street – past the Sherlock Holmes Museum – to Baker Street tube station. If you fancy a pint or bite to eat after your exertions, **The Volunteer** 34, a few metres before the museum, is a good choice.

The Awakening

This marks the end of this walk, but before departing take a look at John Doubleday's (1999) 9.8ft (3m) bronze statue of **Sherlock Holmes** 35, located outside Baker Street tube station on Marylebone Road.

St John's Lodge Garden

An exquisite, quintessentially English garden (just over an acre in size) secreted away down a pergola-draped path and separate from the lodge, St John's is managed and maintained by the Royal Parks and has been open to the public since 1928. It was designed by Robert Weir Schultz in 1892 for the 3rd Marquess of Bute (1847-1900) as a venue 'fit for meditation'. The garden has formal areas, a fountain pond, statues, a Doric temple, stone portico and a partly sunken chapel, reflecting the Arts and Crafts ideas popular at the time. New planting in the '90s further enhanced the garden, which is an unexpected treat.

Sherlock Holmes

START
Hyde Park
Corner tube

See enlarged
detail

PARK LANE

PICCADILLY

KNIGHTSBRIDGE

CONSTITUTION HILL

GROSVENOR CRESCENT

GROSVENOR PLACE

UPPER BELGRAVE STREET

BELGRAVE PLACE

GROSVENOR GDNS

ROAD

VICTORIA STREET

BUCKINGHAM PALACE ROAD

VAUXHALL

WARWICK WAY

BELGRAVE ROAD

10 Belgrave Square

11 1st Marquess of Westminster

12 Simón Bolívar

13 Christopher Columbus

14 Don José de San Martín

15 Prince Henry the Navigator

16 Homage to Leonardo

17 George Basevi

18 Lioness and Lesser Kudu

19 Rifle Brigade Monument

20 Ferdinand Foch

21 Victoria Station

22 Aster Restaurant & Café

23 Victoria Palace Theatre

24 Little Ben

25 The Queens Arms

26 Roller Skater

27 William Huskisson

28 The Helmsman

29 River Cut Tide

30 Vauxhall Bridge

31 MI6 Building

32 Locking Piece

33 Mooring Stone

34 Jeté

35 Tate Britain

36 The Death of Dirce

37 Rescue of Andromeda

38 John Everett Millais

39 Imperial Chemical House

40 Queen Mother's Commemorative Fountain

41 Cooling Tower Panels

● Places of Interest   ● Food & Drink

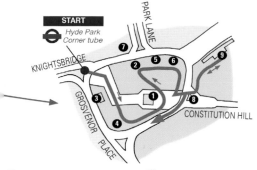

START
Hyde Park
Corner tube

PARK LANE

KNIGHTSBRIDGE

GROSVENOR PLACE

CONSTITUTION HILL

1 Wellington Arch
2 Duke of Wellington
3 Royal Artillery Memorial
4 Australian War Memorial
5 Machine Gun Corps Memorial

6 New Zealand War Memorial
7 Apsley House
8 Memorial Gates
9 RAF Bomber Command Memorial

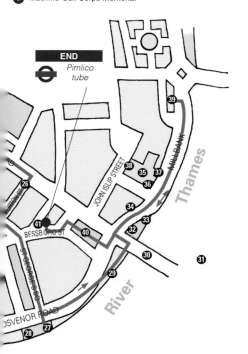

END
Pimlico
tube

MILLBANK

Thames

JOHN ISLIP STREET

BESSBORO ST

River

GROSVENOR ROAD

Hyde Park Corner
to Pimlico

WALK 5

Distance: 4 miles (6½ km)
Terrain: easy
Duration: 2-3 hours
Start: Hyde Park Corner tube
End: Pimlico tube
Postcode: SW1X 7LY

HYDE PARK CORNER TO PIMLICO

One of the busiest junctions in London, Hyde Park Corner – a mega traffic island just southeast of Hyde Park – has a profusion of military memorials, including several to the 1st Duke of Wellington, whose former home, Apsley House, stands serenely alongside the drone of 21st-century traffic. The island is dominated by the Wellington (or Constitution) Arch, originally planned as a northern gateway to the grounds of Buckingham Palace.

Duke of Wellington

From Hyde Park Corner we head west to Belgravia, one of London's most prestigious districts, where Belgrave Square is home to a host of embassies – and not a few sculptures. The area takes its name from one of the Duke of Westminster's subsidiary titles, Viscount Belgrave, which is in turn derived from Belgrave, a village near the Duke's country estate of Eaton Hall in Cheshire. Much of Belgravia is still owned by the Duke of Westminster's family property company, the Grosvenor Estate.

From Belgravia the route goes south to Victoria, one of London's busiest transport interchanges. And from Victoria we continue southeast to Pimlico, known for its lovely garden squares and Regency architecture, developed by the eminent Victorian master builder Thomas Cubitt. Now a conservation area, the district is scattered with monuments and sculptures, not least on the Thames at Millbank, where you can take in the celebrated Tate Britain gallery before heading for Pimlico tube and home.

Hyde Park Corner to Pimlico

Start Walking…

Leaving Hyde Park Corner tube station, cross the road to the large 'island' in the middle of this busy traffic intersection, which contains a number of imposing monuments to triumph and loss in warfare over two centuries. The largest and most impressive is the **Wellington Arch** ❶ (see box), built in 1826-30 to commemorate Wellington's victory over Napoleon at the Battle of Waterloo in 1815. Between the Arch and Apsley House is Sir

Joseph Edgar Boehm's (1888) bronze equestrian statue of the **Duke of Wellington** ❷, set on a polished pink granite plinth. It depicts the Iron Duke in uniform on his favourite horse, Copenhagen, with bronze figures of soldiers from various regiments at each corner.

The island contains a number of other fine memorials. On the western side is the moving **Royal Artillery Memorial** ❸ by Charles Sergeant Jagger (who served with the regiment) and Lionel Pearson, unveiled in 1925. Featuring a giant sculpture of a 9.2-inch howitzer upon a large plinth, surrounded by four bronze figures of artillery men, it includes the disturbing figure of a dead soldier covered by a greatcoat. In the southwest corner of the island is Janet Lawrence's (2003) **Australian War Memorial** ❹, dedicated to the 102,000 Australians who died in the First and Second World Wars. It consists of a semi-circular curved granite wall inscribed with the names of almost 24,000 Australian towns and villages where the soldiers were born; in summer, water runs down over the names, intended to evoke 'memories of service, suffering and sacrifice'.

Wellington Arch

Designed by Decimus Burton, this neoclassical Corinthian triumphal arch was originally crowned with a massive statue of the Duke that stood 28ft (8.5m) high and weighed 40 tonnes; it attracted ridicule as its vast size made the Arch look like a footstool, and was moved to its current location in Aldershot, Hampshire, some years after the Duke's death. The arch gained a new embellishment in 1912: Adrian Jones' large bronze quadriga – a chariot drawn by four horses – is Europe's largest bronze sculpture, depicting the angel of peace descending on the chariot of war. In contrast to its flamboyant decoration, the Portland stone arch is surprisingly plain. The Arch is now owned by English Heritage and visitors can climb to the top (fee), where there are terraces on both sides affording panoramic views, while creative floodlighting makes it an impressive sight at night. (See www.english-heritage.org.uk/visit/places/wellington-arch for information.)

Walk 5

In the north of the island is Francis Derwent Wood's **Machine Gun Corps Memorial** ❺, aka The Boy David, featuring a 9ft (2.7m) bronze statue of a beautiful naked David, with one hand on his hip and the other resting on Goliath's oversized sword. To either side, on a lower flanking plinth of Mazzona marble, is a bronze model of a Vickers machine gun, wreathed in laurels. Finally, in the northeast corner, is

Apsley House

Apsley House

Also known as Number 1 London, Apsley House was the first house visitors saw when passing through the tollgate at Knightsbridge. It was originally built for Lord Apsley by Robert Adam in 1771-8 and was acquired in 1817 by the Duke of Wellington, who faced the red brick walls in Bath stone. Grade I listed and run by English Heritage, it's now a museum and art gallery (Wed-Sun, 11am-5pm, weekends only in summer). The interior has changed little since the Iron Duke's time and is a dazzling example of Regency style. There's also a fine art collection, including works by Brueghel the Elder, Goya, Landseer, Murillo, Rubens, Van Dyck and Velasquez. (For information see www.english-heritage.org.uk/visit/places/apsley-house.)

west towards Piccadilly and Hyde Park for a good view of attractive, honey-coloured **Apsley House** ❼ (see box), the former home of the Duke of Wellington.

From the traffic island, head east and cross the road at the lights opposite Constitution Hill – where three attempts were made on Queen Victoria's life in the 1840s – to reach the pillars of the (Commonwealth) **Memorial Gates** ❽. Designed by Liam O'Connor and inaugurated in 2002, they're inscribed: 'In memory of the five million volunteers from the Indian sub-continent, Africa and the Caribbean who fought with Britain in the two World Wars'. Go left for a short detour along the northern edge of Green Park, where around

Paul Dibble's **New Zealand War Memorial** ❻, commemorating NZ soldiers who fell in the two World Wars. Unveiled in 2006, it consists of 16 bronze X beams (or 'standards') – adorned with texts, patterns and sculptures, symbolic of New Zealand – six of which are arranged in the shape of the Southern Cross constellation. From here, look

RAF Bomber Command Memorial

Hyde Park Corner to Pimlico

100m along on the left is the magnificent – and long overdue – **RAF Bomber Command Memorial**  . Unveiled in 2012 by HM the Queen in her Diamond Jubilee year, it commemorates the sacrifice of 55,573 aircrew servicemen, from Britain, Canada, Czechoslovakia, Poland and other Commonwealth countries, who lost their lives during air-raids in the Second World War. The

Simón Bolívar

monument features Philip Jackson's striking 9ft (2.7m) bronze depicting aircrew returning from a bombing mission. The roof incorporates sections of aluminium recovered from a Handley Page Halifax III bomber shot down over Belgium in May 1944, in which eight Canadian crewmen were killed.

Return to Hyde Park Corner, walk to the southwestern side of the island and cross Grosvenor Place to Grosvenor Crescent, which leads to **Belgrave Square** ❿ . Designed by George Basevi and laid out by Thomas Cubitt in the 1820s, it's one of London's grandest and largest 19th-century squares (covering 4.5 acres/1.82ha) and is the centrepiece of Belgravia. Just north of the square you pass Jonathan Wylder's statue of **Robert Grosvenor, 1st Marquess of Westminster** ⓫ (1767-1845), who was largely responsible for the development of Belgravia. Situated on the small island formed by Grosvenor and Wilton Crescents, the characterful bronze unveiled in 1998 shows Sir Robert holding a scroll (or architectural plan) with his foot on a milestone flanked by two Talbot hunting dogs. On the statue is a quotation

Food & Drink

㉒ Aster Restaurant & Café: A restaurant, café, bar and deli rolled into one, serving breakfast, dinner and everything in between (020-3875 5555, 7am-10.45pm, Sat 9am-10.45pm, Sun 9am-4pm, £-££).

㉕ The Queens Arms: This elegant gastropub caters for all-comers, from carnivores to vegans (020-7834 3313, noon-11pm, £).

㉟ Rex Whistler Restaurant: British classic cuisine in an arty setting in Tate Britain; it's worth a visit just to see Whistler's massive mural, *The Expedition in Pursuit of Rare Meats* (020-7887 8825, lunch only, noon-3pm, £-££)

Walk 5

by John Ruskin: 'When we build, let us think we build for ever'.

The square is home to some fine sculptures, including a rare collection of modern figurative works, many by foreign sculptors, reflecting the international nature of the square's occupants. There are four bronze statues at the corners of the central fenced area, which is a private garden for local residents. In the eastern corner is Hugo Daini's (1973) statue of **Simón Bolívar** ⓬ (1783-1830). An Italian by birth, Bolívar was a Venezuelan military and political leader who played a leading role in the establishment of Venezuela, Bolivia, Colombia, Ecuador, Peru and Panama as sovereign states, free from Spanish rule. The inscription on the plinth reads: 'I am convinced that England alone is capable of protecting

Homage to Leonardo

the world's rights as she is great, glorious and wise'. In the southern corner is a bronze of another Italian, **Christopher Columbus** ⓭ (1451-1506, see box), by Tomás Bañuelos (1992).

In the northern corner (opposite Halkin Street) is Juan Carlos Ferraro's (1993) bronze of **Don José de San Martín** ⓮ (1778-1850), father of Argentine independence, who also gave freedom to Chile and Peru. The fourth statue in the western corner (opposite West Halkin Street) is of **Prince Henry the Navigator** ⓯ (1394-1460) by Simões de Almeida – the only statue of a Portuguese personage in London. It depicts the seated explorer staring off into the distance 'dreaming of far-off lands', holding an unrolling map or scroll in his left hand, wearing a wide brimmed hat, and enveloped in a robe that drapes over his arms, upper body and legs. There are two further sculptures in the gardens in the private fenced-off area. **Homage to Leonardo** ⓰ is a representation of Vitruvian Man, a drawing by Leonardo

---

Christopher Columbus Statue

A gift from the people of Spain, the statue portrays the famous explorer – credited with having 'discovered' the Americas – seated in a chair, one elbow resting on the arm, the other extended and holding a folded and tied map. Columbus is portrayed as a young man, beardless, wearing a cap over his long hair, looking like a romantic hero. The statue is 'dedicated to all the peoples of the Americas in commemoration of the 500th anniversary of the encounter of the two worlds'.

da Vinci. It's a fine work by Italian sculptor Enzo Plazzotta, completed posthumously by his assistant Mark Holloway in 1982 and installed in 1984. Also in the central area is Jonathan Wylder's (2000) bust of **George Basevi** 🔟 (1794-1845), the architect of Belgrave Square.

From the eastern corner of Belgrave Square take Upper Belgrave Street to Eaton Square, and turn left along Hobart Place, bearing right into Upper Grosvenor Garden. The garden retains three pairs of mid-19th-century gate piers and rich wrought-iron gates bearing the Grosvenor monogram. In the centre of the garden is Jonathan Kenworthy's superb bronze of a life-size **Lioness and Lesser Kudu** 🔟, commissioned by the Duke of Westminster. The original was created in 1993 for a lake at Eaton Hall (Cheshire) and a second casting was installed here to mark the opening of the garden to the public in 2000. In the north-eastern corner is John Tweed's (1924) **Rifle Brigade Monument** 🔟, depicting soldiers from the 19th and 20th centuries around a central inscription to those who fell in the Great War.

From Upper Grosvenor Garden walk along Grosvenor Gardens to Lower Grosvenor Garden, where at the southern end is Georges Malissard's superb bronze

Victoria Station

One of London's historic grand mainline stations, Victoria began life as two separate (unconnected) stations for the London, Brighton & South Coast Railway (LB&SCR) and the London Chatham & Dover Railway (LC&DR). The Brighton station opened in 1860, with the Chatham station following two years later in 1862, when the grand Grosvenor Hotel was built. The two stations came largely under single ownership in 1923, with the formation of the Southern Railway. The combined station was immediately popular as a London terminus and noted for its luxury Pullman train services and continental boat train trips – nowadays it serves Gatwick Airport via the Gatwick Express. Victoria is also the venue for London's principal coach (long distance buses) station.

equestrian statue of French general **Ferdinand Foch** 🔟. The

Lioness & Lesser Kudu

Supreme Commander of Allied Forces on the Western Front in spring 1918, Foch was acclaimed as the architect of Germany's ultimate defeat and surrender in November 1918. His statue faces **Victoria Station** 🔟 (see box above), but you cross

Buckingham Palace Road and head east down Victoria Street, where you're spoilt for choice for places to eat. One of our favourites is the **Aster Restaurant & Café** 22 at number 150, which offers a delicious Nordic-French menu.

Further along Victoria Street is the **Victoria Palace Theatre** 23 , designed by leading theatre architect Frank Matcham and opened in 1911. On the cupola above the theatre is a lovely gilded ballerina (artist unknown), below which are two semi-clad stone muses. Opposite the theatre is **Little Ben** 24 , a cast-iron miniature clock tower erected in 1892 and modelled on the famous original (known colloquially as Big Ben) in the Palace of Westminster. From Victoria Street go right down Vauxhall Bridge Road towards Pimlico. If you still haven't eaten, there are some good options here. Check out **The Queens Arms** 25 (turn right on Warwick Way and walk one block down on the right), a Victorian gastropub, or try The

Warwick, another gastropub a few doors further along. Return to Vauxhall Bridge Road and, at the entrance to Moreton Street, you'll see André Wallace's (2010) statue of a **Roller**

Roller Skater

Skater 26 . Turn right along Moreton Street and left on St George's Square, and go straight across at the junction with Lupus Street to continue along the square past the church of St Saviour's Pimlico. A long narrow garden square, St George's has had many notable residents, including Dracula author Bram Stoker (1847-1912), who lived and died at number 26.

At the southern end of the square is Pimlico Gardens overlooking the Thames, which contains John Gibson's fine marble statue of **William Huskisson** 27 (1770-1830). A 19th-century Member of Parliament, Huskisson has the unfortunate distinction of being the first person in the world to be run over and killed by a railway engine – George Stephenson's locomotive engine Rocket, no less – in 1830. Here he's depicted wearing a classical drape in toga fashion, looking more like a Roman senator than a British MP. Also in the garden is **The Helmsman** 28 , another André Wallace bronze. Donated by Berkeley Homes and installed in 1996, it depicts a small stylised, male figure at the helm of a boat, and reflects the fact that ships once sailed from near here.

William Huskisson

Hyde Park Corner to Pimlico

MI6 Building

From the park head right along Grosvenor Road and, after around 50m, take the Thames Path, where you see Paul Mason's **River Cut Tide** 29, a nondescript abstract short marble column. Large Art Deco-style lamps decorate the wall along this part of the riverbank. Continue along the path to **Vauxhall Bridge** 30 (see box), which is decorated with bronze figures on its arches by Frederick William Pomeroy and Alfred Drury; those on the upstream side represent Pottery, Engineering, Architecture and Agriculture, while Science, Fine Arts, Local Government and Education feature downstream.

Vauxhall Bridge

Originally called Regent's Bridge, the first Vauxhall Bridge was opened by the Prince Regent in 1816 and was a toll bridge (charges ceased in 1879). One of London's most attractive and colourful bridges, today's Vauxhall Bridge (Grade II* listed) was designed by Sir Alexander Binnie in 1895 and opened in 1906. The bridge features five steel arches on granite piers and was the first in London to carry trams.

At the end of the path climb the stairs to Vauxhall Bridge and cross the road at the traffic lights to Millbank, from where there's a good view of the imposing **MI6 Building** 31 on the opposite bank. Opened in 1994, it's an ostentatious pile with echoes of Egyptian pyramids and Mayan temples; indeed, it has been nicknamed the Aztec Temple, although it has also been less flatteringly dubbed the Ceauşescu Tower, after the late Romanian dictator's fondness for large, self-aggrandising building schemes. Designed by postmodernist architect Terry Farrell, it houses the Secret Intelligence Service (SIS), better known as MI6, dealing with overseas intelligence.

A short way along Millbank you come to Riverside Walk Gardens, where you'll find Henry Moore's bronze, **Locking Piece** 32, a 1964 work installed here in 1968, displayed on a granite plinth at the northern tip of the gardens. Close by is a cylindrical **Mooring Stone** 33 or bollard (with an inscription) where penitentiary ships used to tie up. It's a grim reminder of Millbank Prison (1816-1890) – now demolished – which served as a holding facility for convicted prisoners before they were transported to Australia. Almost opposite the Moore work – on the corner, just before a small cul-de-sac – is Enzo Plazzotta's beautiful bronze dancer **Jeté** 34, unveiled in 1985. The elegant statue depicts the dancer David

Walk 5

Wall making his soaring entrance in the ballet La Bayadère, in full flight with a trailing cloth anchoring him to the pedestal.

Jeté

Continue for around 100m to **Tate Britain** ⑤ (see box opposite). On the pediment of the Millbank entrance is a statue of Britannia (sculptor unknown), flanked by a lion and a unicorn. To the left of the entrance is Charles Bennett Lawes-Wittewronge's **The Death of Dirce** ㊱ , based on the Farnese Bull, a classical sculpture depicting the fate of the wife of the King of Thebes, who was tied to the horns of a wild bull. It was presented to the Tate by the sculptor's widow in 1911. On the other side of the entrance is the bronze **Rescue of Andromeda** ㊲ by Henry Charles Fehr (1893). It depicts the moment when, according to Greek legend, the hero Perseus (the son of Zeus and Danae) saves the beautiful Andromeda from being devoured by a sea monster. At the rear of the gallery in John Islip Street – where it was relegated in 2000 – stands Thomas Brock's bronze of **John Everett Millais** ㊳ (1829-96) on a carved stone pedestal. One of the best-known Victorian painters, Millais was one of the founders of the pre-Raphaelite

Brotherhood's pre-Impressionist genre of painting.

Continue along Millbank, past Tate Britain and Thames House (home of MI5, the UK Security Service), to **Imperial Chemical House** ㊴ (number 9 Millbank), opposite Lambeth Bridge. It was designed by Sir Frank Baines in neoclassical style and built between 1927 and 1929 for the newly created Imperial Chemical Industries (ICI). The three main façades are decorated with giant niches spanning the fourth and fifth storeys, each with a set-back window topped by a peacock sculpture and an arched light above with a portrait keystone by William Bateman Fagan. There are eight in total and each dedicated to a different chemist – their names are carved on the balcony below. Above the fifth storey is an entablature, with a balustrade on the parapet above bearing superb allegorical figures in Portland stone by Charles Sargeant Jagger, representing construction, marine transport, agriculture and chemistry. The massive bronze doors on the ground floor entrance, also by Fagan, are worth a look, with relief panels illustrating the

Rescue of Andromeda

evelopment of science and echnology.

Retrace your steps to Vauxhall Bridge Road and cross over to Bessborough Gardens, where you'll find the **Queen Mother's Commemorative Fountain** ④⓪ , designed by Sir Peter Shepheard and installed in 1980. It features a pair of intertwined sturgeons (often mistaken for dolphins), an aluminium cast from one of George Vulliamy's 'dolphin' standard lamps along the Thames Embankment. Leave the gardens and go left to Drummond Gate and Bessborough Street, where Pimlico tube station – and the end of this walk – is on the right. Before departing, take a few minutes to admire Eduardo Paolozzi's cast-iron **Cooling Tower Panels** ④① outside the station: decorated relief panels encase the cooling equipment for

the tube station's air-conditioning and are described by the architects as 'an opportunity to transform a mechanical necessity into a genuine sculpture'.

Tate Britain

This is the original Tate Gallery, opened in 1897 to provide a dedicated home for British art. A major rebranding in 2000 saw its modern art moved downriver to Tate Modern at Bankside, while Tate Britain, as it's now known, displays historic and contemporary art. The gallery's permanent collection dates from 1500 to the present day, and is one of the most comprehensive of its kind in the world, including major works by Turner, Gainsborough, Hogarth, Constable, Stubbs, Bacon, Moore, Hockney and many more. The gallery's Rex Whistler Restaurant is well worth a visit. (See www.tate.org. uk/tate_britain for information.)

Tate Britain

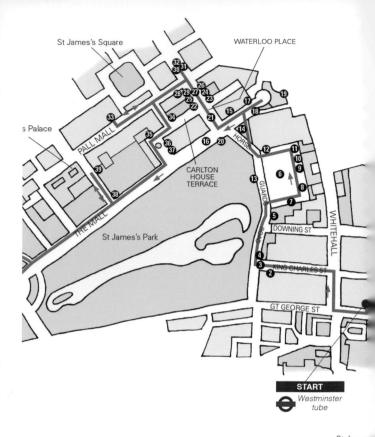

St James's Square

WATERLOO PLACE

s Palace

PALL MALL

CARLTON HOUSE TERRACE

THE MALL

St James's Park

HORSE

GUARDS

DOWNING ST

KING CHARLES ST

WHITEHALL

GT GEORGE ST

START
Westminster tube

St James

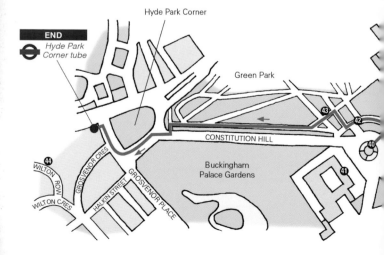

Hyde Park Corner

END
Hyde Park Corner tube

Green Park

CONSTITUTION HILL

Buckingham Palace Gardens

GROSVENOR CRES

GROSVENOR PLACE

HALKIN STREET

WILTON ROW

WILTON CRES

WALK 6

● Places of Interest   Food & Drink

Westminster to Hyde Park Corner

Walk 6

Distance: 2½ miles (4 km)
Terrain: easy
Duration: 1½–2 hours
Start: Westminster tube
End: Hyde Park Corner tube
Postcode: SW1A 2JR

There's a military theme to this walk, which takes in many monuments to the great and the good from conflicts of the last two centuries – including the Crimean, Boer and two World Wars – as well as icons of empire and monarchy. We start in Westminster, at the Churchill War Rooms – the underground bunker from where Winston Churchill and his war cabinet directed the Second World War against Nazi Germany – and from there head to Horse Guards Parade. Formerly the site of the Palace of Westminster's tiltyard, nowadays Horse Guards is the venue for the annual Trooping the Colour ceremony, which commemorates the monarch's official birthday (second Saturday in June). Not surprisingly, the parade is awash with military memorials and statues.

From Horse Guards we go north to The Mall, which runs from Admiralty Arch to Buckingham Palace. North of The Mall is St James's Palace, built between 1531 and 1536 by Henry VIII and the primary residence of British monarchs until 1837, when Queen Victoria made Buckingham Palace her official home. After making a short detour to see the many splendid monuments and statues in Waterloo Place, we return to The Mall to admire the Victoria Memorial, one of London's most spectacular monuments.

From here it's a short stroll along Constitution Hill – where Charles II took his 'constitutional' walks – skirting Green Park, to Hyde Park Corner and the end of the walk.

Horse Guards Parade

Westminster to Hyde Park Corner

Start Walking...

Exit Westminster tube station – there's a **Caffè Nero** 1 next door if you fancy a coffee – and go right along Bridge Street, right again down Parliament Street and left into King Charles Street. At the end of the street, at the top of Clive Steps and adjacent to the **Churchill War Rooms** 2 (see box), is John Tweed's (1912) statue of **Robert Clive** 3 (1725-1774), better known as Clive of India. Clive was Commander-in-Chief of British India and was credited with establishing the military and political supremacy of the East India Company in Bengal, in addition to securing a large swathe of South Asia (today's India, Pakistan and Bangladesh) to generate wealth for the company. He reportedly committed suicide in 1774 at the age of 49 after a failed attempt to impeach him by the House of Commons. Nearby, at the bottom right of Clive Steps, is Martin Cook and Gary Breeze's (2006) **Bali Memorial** 4 , commemorating the 202 victims of the terrorist bombings on the Indonesian island in 2002. The victims' names are listed on a Portland stone wall, in front of which stands a granite globe with 202 doves etched into its surface.

Go right along Horse Guards Road where, just after Downing Street on a small green (no access) is Czech Franta Belsky's 1983 bronze of **Lord Louis Mountbatten** 5 (1900-1979), 1st Earl Mountbatten of Burma. Mountbatten – who was murdered by the IRA in Ireland in 1979 – is

Churchill War Rooms

A branch of the Imperial War Museum, the Churchill War Rooms (entrance fee, 9.30am-6pm) comprise the Cabinet War Rooms and the Churchill Museum, devoted to the life of Sir Winston Churchill. The Cabinet War Rooms became operational in August 1939, shortly before the outbreak of war, and were the nerve centre of Britain's war effort, equipped with accommodation, offices, communications and broadcasting equipment, sound-proofing, ventilation and reinforcement. (See www.iwm.org.uk/visits/churchill-war-rooms for information.)

depicted in the uniform of Admiral of the Fleet, wearing his Order of the Garter and holding binoculars. Just past Mountbatten, turn right and on the southern edge of **Horse Guards Parade** 6 (see box, page 74) is John Tweed's 1926 statue of **Lord Kitchener** 7 (1850-1916). Field Marshal Horatio Herbert Kitchener won notoriety for his imperial

Bali Memorial

Walk 6

Cádiz Memorial

campaigns and his establishment of concentration camps during the Second Boer War in Africa. He was Secretary of State for War in 1914 and was the face of the recruitment poster ('Your Country Needs YOU') for the largest volunteer army Britain had seen. He was killed in 1916 when *HMS Hampshire* struck a mine off Orkney and sank with the loss of 737 lives.

From Kitchener's statue walk around the perimeter of the parade anti-clockwise to Dover House (Grade I listed), in front of which is the **Cádiz Memorial** ❽ . This impressive monument by Robert Shipster depicts a large

brass sculpture of the monster Geryon – from Greek mythology but also associated with the Isle of Gades on which Cádiz stands – its twin tails twisting round the mortar which it supports on its back. The mortar was presented to the Prince Regent after the British helped lift the siege of Cádiz by the French in 1812. The next work on the parade is Henry Poole's (1924) superb equestrian statue of **Field Marshal Earl Roberts** ❾ (1832-1914). One of the most successful military commanders of the 19th century, he served in India, Abyssinia (modern-day Ethiopia) and Afghanistan, before

Field Marshal Roberts

leading British forces to success in the Second Boer War. The final figurative work here is another equestrian statue, **Field Marshal Lord Wolseley** ❿ (1833-1913), by Sir William Goscombe John, unveiled in 1920. Wolseley was a contemporary of Roberts, and equally admired, although it's said the two generals couldn't stand one another. A little further along is the **Ottoman Gun** ⓫ (see box opposite).

Continuing around the parade you come to the **Royal Naval Division Memorial Fountain** ⓬ in the northwest corner, dedicated to the 45,000 members of the division who died in the First

---

Horse Guards Parade

In the days of Henry VIII this was a tiltyard, where jousting tournaments took place, but nowadays Horse Guards Parade is the venue for the annual ceremonies of Trooping the Colour and Beating Retreat. The latter is a spectacular evening pageant of music and military precision drill, including horses, cannon and fireworks, held on the Wednesday and Thursday evenings prior to Trooping the Colour ceremony in June.

Westminster to Hyde Park Corner

World War at Gallipoli and on the Western Front. Designed by Sir Edwin Lutyens and erected in 1925, it contains a sonnet by Rupert Brooke (1887-1915), who died on active service with the Royal Naval Division in the Dardanelles. On the western edge of Horse Guards Parade in St James's Park is Gilbert Ledward's **Guards Memorial** ⑬ (1926), commemorating the guardsmen who died in the Great War. In the form of a cenotaph, it features five life-size bronze figures each representing one of the five Foot Guards' Regiments (Grenadiers, Coldstream, Scots, Welsh and Irish).

Continue north along Horse Guards Road, where in the small triangle in the right-hand corner, is the **National Police Memorial** ⑭ by Lord Foster of Thames Bank and Per Arnoldi, unveiled in 2005. It commemorates some 4,000 police officers killed in the course of their duties in the UK (since 1792). The memorial consists of a black rectangular creeper-covered tablet, containing an inscribed roll of honour behind a glass panel, and a separate blue glass column sited in a reflecting pool linked by a terrace of Purbeck stone.

Ottoman Gun

Captured by the British after the siege of Alexandria during the Napoleonic Wars in 1801, this magnificent gun was installed in Horse Guards Parade the following year. The embossed barrel was made by Murad (the son of the Ottoman army's chief gunner) in 1524, while the gun carriage – also richly decorated – is British-made and much later. Egypt was conquered by the Turks in 1517 and this gun would have been used at the decisive Battle of Mohács in Hungary in 1526, when the forces of the Ottoman Empire led by Suleiman the Magnificent defeated a combined force of Hungarians and Serbians, leaving the way open for them to lay siege (unsuccessfully) to Vienna.

If you're ready for lunch, then the **Rochelle Canteen** 15 in the Institute of Contemporary Arts, just opposite the memorial, is recommended.

From the police memorial go right along **The Mall** ⑯ (see box, page 76), where around 100m up on the left (outside the Mall Galleries and just before Admiralty Arch) is the superb **Royal Marines Memorial** ⑰ , aka the Graspan Memorial, a bronze sculpture by Adrian Jones (1903). It originally commemorated the Royal Marines who died in the Boxer rebellion in China and in the Second Boer War in Africa (Graspan is where the main battle was fought in Northern Cape, South Africa), but

The Mall

The Mall began life as a field for playing pall-mall (a precursor to croquet) and in the 17th and 18th centuries was a fashionable promenade bordered by trees. It was envisioned as a ceremonial route in the early 20th century, matching the creation of similar routes in other major world cities. The surface of The Mall is coloured red to give the effect of a giant red carpet leading to Buckingham Palace. Scheduled buses are prohibited from using The Mall or passing Buckingham Palace without permission of the monarch – which has only been given twice, in 1927 and 1950 – and is closed to all traffic on Sundays, public holidays and ceremonial occasions.

in 2000 was rededicated to all fallen marines. Opposite, on the other side of The Mall, is Thomas Brock's (1914) statue of **Captain James Cook 18** (1728-1779). The inscription on the plinth reads: 'Circumnavigator of the globe, explorer of the Pacific Ocean, he laid the foundations of the British Empire in Australia and New Zealand, chartered the shores of Newfoundland and traversed the ocean gates of Canada, both east and west'.

A bit further along is **Admiralty Arch 19**, designed by Sir Aston Webb and completed in 1912, formerly the official residence of the First Sea Lord (there are plans to convert it into a hotel). Look for the sculptural figures by Thomas Brock at the ends of the two wings, representing Navigation (left) and Gunnery (right). On the inside wall of the northernmost arch at a height of around 7ft (2.1m) is a plaster nose (yes a nose!) by Rick Buckley, one of a number of casts of the artist's nose installed around London.

Retrace your steps along The Mall and just past Horse Guards Road, on the left, is the **Royal Artillery Boer War Memorial 20** by William Robert Colton, unveiled in 1910. It commemorates members of the Royal Artillery killed in the Second Boer War in southern Africa 1899-1902. The memorial features a bronze winged figure of Peace subduing a horse representing War, on a pedestal of Portland stone designed by Sir Aston Webb. The pillars at each end are mounted with six bronze panels, two of which carry relief depictions of the war. Opposite the RA memorial, ascend the Duke of York Steps to the **Duke of York Column 21** (see

Admiralty Arch

Westminster to Hyde Park Corner

Food & Drink

1 Caffè Nero: The ubiquitous chain's branch at Westminster tube station is a good place to grab a coffee (6am-9.30pm, Sun from 7am, £)

15 Rochelle Canteen: Restaurant and bar in the Institute of Contemporary Arts with a changing seasonal menu (Tue-Sun 11am-11pm, lunch noon-3pm, dinner 6-10pm, closed Mon, £).

44 The Grenadier: Historic Greene King pub in a tiny former officers' mess with good ales and pub grub (020-7235 3074, 11am-11.30pm, £).

Duke of York Column

At 138ft (42m) this is one of London's tallest monuments and commemorates Prince Frederick, Duke of York (1763-1827), the second-eldest son of George III. On top of the Tuscan column – designed by Benjamin Dean Wyatt – is a plinth bearing Sir Richard Westmacott's bronze of the duke, dressed in the robes of a Knight of the Garter. The Duke's memorial was financed by docking a day's pay (involuntarily) from every soldier in the British army. Once completed, the great height of the column caused contemporary wits to suggest that the Duke was trying to escape his creditors, as he died £2 million in debt (around £150 million today!).

box), erected in 1832, while the statue was installed in 1834.

Just beyond the column, Waterloo Place has an abundance of commemorative statuary. On the left-hand corner (with Carlton House Terrace) is Edgar Boehm's bronze (1877) of Field Marshal **John Fox Burgoyne 22** (1782-1871), who distinguished himself in many battles of the Peninsular Wars under the Duke of Wellington, while on the right is **Sir John Lawrence 23** (1811-1879), also by Boehm (1885), who was chief administrator of

the Punjab during the Indian Mutiny and Viceroy of India 1864-69. Just past Lawrence on the right-hand side of Waterloo Place is Carlo Marochetti's (1867) bronze of **Field Marshal Lord Clyde 24** (1792-1863), which depicts Britannia seated on a British 'lion couchant', resting her sword against the lion's flank and extending a symbol of peace. As Colin Campbell, Clyde had a distinguished military career, which included commanding the Highland Brigade at the Battle of Alma during the Crimean War, and bringing the Indian Mutiny to an end in 1858 as Commander-in-Chief of the army.

Walk 6

Almost opposite Clyde, on the other side of Waterloo Place, is a statue of Rear Admiral **Sir John Franklin** 25 (1786-1847) by Matthew Noble (1866). A Royal Navy officer and Arctic explorer, Franklin died attempting to navigate and chart a section of the North West Passage in the Canadian Arctic. Facing Franklin is another tragic polar explorer, **Robert Scott** 26 (1868-1912), aka 'Scott of the Antarctic', completed in 1915 by his sculptor widow Kathleen Scott. A British naval captain, Scott led two expeditions to the Antarctic regions, where he died after reaching the South Pole in 1912. Following news of his death, Scott

Edward VII

became a celebrated hero, which is reflected in the many memorials to him erected across the UK.

In the centre of Waterloo Place is an equestrian statue of **Edward VII** 27 (1841-1910) by Australian-born sculptor Bertram Mackennal (1921). To the west of Edward VII, next to the **Athenaeum Club** 28 (see box), is Les Johnston's bronze of **Sir Keith Park** 29 (1892-1975), unveiled in 2010. One of the unsung heroes of the Second World War, New Zealander Air Chief Marshal Park commanded the RAF squadrons that defended London and the South East from Luftwaffe attacks during the Battle of Britain.

Cross Pall Mall to continue along Waterloo Place, where there's a trio of memorials linked by a common theme. On the left is Arthur George Walker's (1915) bronze of **Florence Nightingale** 30 (1820-1910 – see box, right), the founder of modern nursing. Note the four superb plaques depicting scenes from her work during the Crimean War. Alongside Nightingale is John Henry Foley's (1867) bronze of **Sidney Herbert** 31

Athenaeum Club

A private members' club founded in 1824, the Athenaeum has an impressive neoclassical clubhouse, designed by Decimus Burton (1800-1881) when he was just 24 and already an acclaimed architect. The building has a Doric portico, above which is a statue of the classical goddess of wisdom, Athena (or Pallas Athene) by Edward Hodges Bailey, from whom the club derives its name. The bas-relief frieze by John Henning is a copy of the frieze of the Parthenon in Athens, aka the 'Elgin Marbles', now (controversially) in the British Museum.

Westminster to Hyde Park Corner

Florence Nightingale

One of Britain's greatest heroines, Nightingale came to prominence while serving as a manager of nurses trained by her during the Crimean War, where the Turkish lantern she carried earned her the sobriquet 'The Lady with the Lamp'. She was a visionary health reformer, a brilliant campaigner and the second most influential woman in Victorian Britain after Queen Victoria. The Nightingale Pledge taken by new nurses was named in her honour, and International Nurses Day is still celebrated throughout the world on her birthday (12th May).

(1810-1861), 1st Baron Herbert of Lea, a British statesman who was a close ally and confident of Florence Nightingale. It was Herbert who sent Nightingale to Scutari Barracks in Istanbul (where she established her hospital during the Crimean War), and with her he led the movement for reform of the War Office's medical services after the war. Just behind stands the **Guards Crimean War Memorial** 32 by John Bell, commemorating the Allied victory in the Crimean War (1853–56). Unveiled in 1861, it includes statues of three Guardsmen, with a female allegorical figure referred to as Honour, cast in bronze from cannons captured at the Siege of Sevastopol.

From the Guards Memorial go right and walk southwest on Pall Mall to the Army & Navy Club, just past St James's Square. Here, secured in a glass case, is Basil Gotto's (1926) **Army & Navy Club War Memorial** 33. Retrace your steps along Pall Mall and go right on Carlton Gardens to Carlton House Terrace, where on the left-hand corner is Sir Bertram Mackennal's fine statue of **Lord Curzon** 34 (1859-1925), unveiled in 1931, facing his former home at 1 Carlton House Terrace. He was the last great Victorian Viceroy of India from 1899 to1905 and creator of the territory of Eastern Bengal and Assam, but his political ambitions ultimately ended in failure. Turn right along Carlton Gardens, where tucked away on the right, is a statue of **General de Gaulle** 35 (1890-1970) opposite the building where he established the Free French Forces HQ during the Second World War. The bronze statue by Angela Conner was unveiled in 1993 and shows a typically defiant de Gaulle in the uniform of a General de Brigade.

Opposite de Gaulle, between Carlton Gardens and The Mall, are statues of **George VI** 36 (1895-1952) and **Queen Elizabeth, the**

George VI & Queen Elizabeth

Queen Mother ③⑦ (1900-2002), shown right. George VI's bronze statue is by William McMillan, and depicts the king dressed in naval uniform on a Portland stone plinth. The bronze of Queen Elizabeth is by Philip Jackson with a relief sculpture by Paul Day, and shows her at the time she was widowed at the age of 51. Both statues were unveiled by Queen Elizabeth II, in 1955 and 2009 respectively.

Queen Alexandra Memorial

From the statues, go right along The Mall to Marlborough Road. Set into the wall on the right-hand side is William Reid Dick's (1967) memorial to **Queen Mary ③⑧** (1867-1953), wife of George V. Behind the wall is Marlborough House – the London base for the Dukes of Marlborough for over a century, and Queen Mary's home from 1936 until her death. Around 100m up on the right in Marlborough Road is Sir Alfred Gilbert's striking **Queen Alexandra Memorial ③⑨**, commemorating Queen Alexandra of Denmark (1844-1925), wife of Edward VII. Set into the garden wall of Marlborough House, the

memorial – a wonderful example of Art Nouveau style – consists of a bronze screen incorporating allegorical figures.

Return to The Mall and go right, where around 300m along is the magnificent **Queen Victoria Memorial ④⓪** (see box opposite) in front of **Buckingham Palace ④①**. Off to the right is the handsome golden **Canada Gate ④②**, which forms a grand entrance to Green Park and the tree-lined Broad Walk. The gates were a gift from Canada to celebrate its contribution to the British Empire and were installed in 1911 as part of the memorial to Queen Victoria. Designed by Sir Aston Webb, they're in the same style as those of Buckingham Palace and bear the emblems of the seven Canadian provinces at that time. While you're here, it's worth inspecting the palace gates, which are spectacular.

Go left past Canada Gate and enter Green Park via the path in the corner, where around 100m from the gate (over to the right) is the **Canada Memorial ④③**, which commemorates the 113,663 Canadians who died in the two World Wars. Designed by Canadian Pierre Granche and unveiled in 1994, it's made from red granite and divided by a walkway into two distinct halves, representing Britain and Canada's joint participation in the two World Wars. The inclined sculpture is inset with bronze maple leaves (the Canadian emblem) and the country's coat of arms, while water flows across the sloping surface and creates an illusion of floating leaves.

Queen Victoria Memorial

Sculpted by Sir Thomas Brock and unveiled by George V in 1911, this imposing imperial memorial commemorates Queen Victoria (1819-1901) and the glory days of the British Empire. The statue of the Queen is over 18ft (5.5m) high and cut from a single block of white Carrara marble, while the whole monument stands at 82ft (25m) and comprises 2,300 tonnes of marble. Many allegorical figures accompany Victoria, representing courage, constancy, victory, justice, truth and motherhood, among others. The overall design of the monument was conceived by Sir Aston Webb – and includes the Memorial Gardens – a broad semi-circular sweep of flowerbeds enclosed by a low stone balustrade – and the ornamental gates on the roads encircling the monument.

From the Canada Memorial go left and take the path northwest running parallel to Constitution Hill, which takes you to Hyde Park Corner tube station, and the end of the walk. If you fancy a beer or a bite to eat, **The Grenadier 44** in Wilton Row, a few minutes' walk to the west, is a lovely traditional pub with good ales and pub grub.

Winged Victory

Queen Victoria Memorial

Motherhood

Queen Victoria

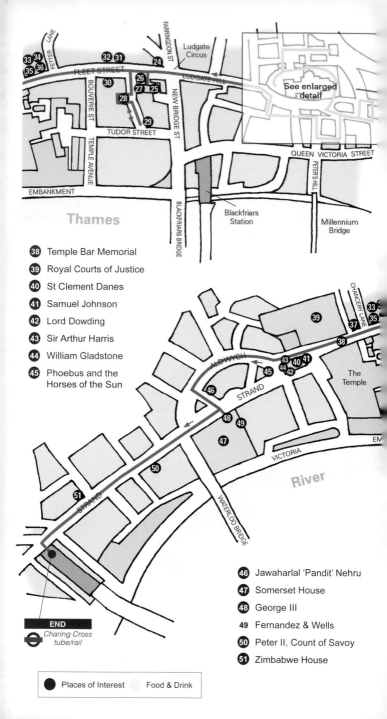

38 Temple Bar Memorial
39 Royal Courts of Justice
40 St Clement Danes
41 Samuel Johnson
42 Lord Dowding
43 Sir Arthur Harris
44 William Gladstone
45 Phoebus and the Horses of the Sun

46 Jawaharlal 'Pandit' Nehru
47 Somerset House
48 George III
49 Fernandez & Wells
50 Peter II, Count of Savoy
51 Zimbabwe House

Places of Interest   Food & Drink

END
Charing Cross
tube/rail

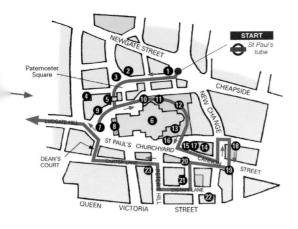

WALK 7

St Paul's to the Strand

Distance: 2¾ miles (4½ km)
Terrain: easy
Duration: 1½-2½ hours
Start: St Paul's tube
End: Charing Cross tube/rail
Postcode: EC2V 6BJ

ST PAUL'S TO THE STRAND

This walk commences in the shadow of St Paul's Cathedral, architect Christopher Wren's masterpiece constructed after the Great Fire of 1666. One of the city's most recognisable sights, it occupies a significant place in the national identity as the Anglican mother church of London and the venue for many Royal celebrations. The cathedral and its surrounds are a popular location for memorials and monuments, not all with religious connotations.

St Paul's Cathedral

The route continues west along two of the city's most famous thoroughfares: Fleet Street and the Strand. Fleet Street gets its name from the River Fleet (which now runs underground) and is the former home of the newspaper industry, which moved out in the '80s. There are monuments and statues along its entire length, and a number honour figures from the British press, including Lord Northcliffe and T. P. O'Connor.

The Strand, in the district of Covent Garden – the name comes from old English *strond*, meaning the edge of the river – was popular with the aristocracy up to the 18th century. In the 19th century it became famous for its coffee shops, restaurants, theatres and music halls – it remains the home of a number of theatres and luxury hotels, including the Savoy. Today, figures as diverse as William Gladstone, Samuel Johnson and Jawaharlal Nehru are commemorated here.

St Paul's to the Strand

Start Walking…

As you leave St Paul's tube station, check out the wall to the left of Caffè Nero in Panyer Alley to see a bas-relief of the **Panyer Boy** ❶. It depicts a naked boy astride a panyer or bread basket (from the French *pannier*) – panyers were made here for bakers in nearby Bread Street. Continue along Panyer Alley and go right down Paternoster Row to Paternoster Square, named after the makers of paternoster prayer beads. Directly ahead as you enter the square is Elisabeth Frink's bronze, **Shepherd and Sheep** ❷, aka Paternoster, unveiled in 1975 by the late violin virtuoso Yehudi Menuhin. The subject of the statue – a shepherd herding five sheep – reflects the former use of Paternoster Row as the site of Newgate Market, where livestock and meat were sold. In the centre of the square is the **Paternoster Square Column** ❸, aka the Flaming Orb Monument, designed by Whitfield Partners. The 75ft (23m) Portland stone Corinthian column is topped by a flaming copper urn covered in gold leaf that's illuminated by fibre-optics at night; the column also has a more practical use as it serves as a ventilation shaft for a service road beneath the square.

Shepherd and Sheep

Temple Bar

This imposing gateway originally stood at the principal ceremonial entrance to the City of London from the City of Westminster (its original location between Fleet Street and the Strand is now marked by the Temple Bar Memorial – see page 91). Temple Bar is first mentioned in 1293, although the gateway you see today is attributed to Sir Christopher Wren and dates from 1672. It contains four statues in niches by John Bushnell: James I (1566-1625), his Queen consort Anne of Denmark (1574-1619), Charles I (1600-1649) and Charles II (1630-1685). The handsome gate marked the gateway to the City for 200 years – it was also where traitors' heads were displayed until 1746 – but was removed in 1878 due to traffic congestion and for a century stood at Theobalds Park in Hertfordshire. It was installed as an entrance to the redeveloped Paternoster Square in 2004.

On the north side of the square in Paternoster Lane is Thomas Heatherwick's **Paternoster Vents** ❹ (aka Angel's Wings), which was installed in 2002 and provides ventilation for an underground electrical substation, while in the southwest corner is **Temple Bar** ❺ (see box).

Go through Temple Bar to Paternoster Row and **St Paul's Cathedral** ❻ (see box on page 86) and its gardens, which contain a number of memorials. Follow Paternoster Row round to the right to the western end of the cathedral, where there's an 1888 reproduction of Francis Bird's 1712 statue of **Queen Anne** **7** (1665-1714) – the reigning monarch when the cathedral was completed. On the **West Façade** **8** of St Paul's behind Queen Anne are a number of other statues by Francis Bird, including the Conversion of St Paul in the west pediment, seven reliefs of scenes from the life of St Paul around the west door, and four seated evangelists at the bases of the two towers. In front of Juxon House (opposite Queen Anne) are Emily Young's (2003) five giant stone **Angel Heads** **9** on columns.

Continue east along Paternoster Row to the cathedral churchyard garden, where immediately on the left is a statue of **John Wesley** **10** (1703-1791), the theologian, cleric and co-founder of Methodism,

John Wesley

depicted wearing a cassock and holding a bible. The statue, erected in 1988, was cast from a sculpture created by Samuel Manning and son between 1825 and 1849. Just past Wesley (outside the cathedral's north transept) is Richard Kindersley's (1999) modest **People of London Memorial** **11**, officially titled the 'Memorial to the Londoners killed in World War Two Bombardments', commemorating over 30,000 Londoners killed during the Blitz (see box opposite). Carved from a three-ton block of Irish limestone, the memorial is set into the paving and has a gilded inscription around the outside which reads, 'Remember before God the people of London 1939-1945'. On the top of the stone, written in a spiral, is an inscription by polymath Sir Edward Marsh (1872-1953): 'In war: resolution, in defeat: defiance, in victory: magnanimity, in peace: goodwill' (words quoted by Winston Churchill in his history, *The Second World War*).

Located in the northeast of the churchyard is **St Paul's Cross** **12**, a Baroque revival design by Sir Reginald Blomfield with a statue of St Paul by Sir Bertram Mackennal (1910) standing on a Doric column of Portland stone. It's erected near the site of the original St Paul's Cross, which was the most important public pulpit in Tudor

---

St Paul's Cathedral

An Anglican cathedral and the seat of the Bishop of London, St Paul's sits atop the City's highest hill (Ludgate). At 365ft (111m) it was, until 1962, the tallest structure in London and its dome still dominates the skyline. Sir Christopher Wren's English Baroque masterpiece is the fifth church to stand here – the first dated from 604AD – built between 1675 and 1710 after its predecessor was destroyed in the Great Fire. The Cathedral (high entrance fee) has a bookshop, café and restaurant.

and early Stuart England. On the south side of the cathedral is Edward Bainbridge Copnall's arresting statue of a falling **Thomas Becket** ⓭ (1119-1170), Archbishop of Canterbury from 1162 until his death. Becket was murdered in Canterbury Cathedral by followers of Henry II, and is venerated as a saint and martyr by both the Catholic and Anglican churches. The statue, which dates from 1970, is resin, coloured to simulate bronze.

Thomas Becket

Exit the churchyard (to the left of Becket) in the southeast corner to the award-winning **Festival Gardens** ⓮ . Designed by Sir Albert Richardson, they were the Corporation of London's contribution to the Festival of Britain in 1951, and now include the adjacent Queen's Diamond Jubilee Garden and Carter Lane Gardens. On the path a few steps ahead is Nigel Boonham's fine bust of **John Donne** ⓯ (1572-1631), unveiled in 2012 and facing east towards his birthplace on Bread Street. Donne was one of England's foremost poets and priests and a former Dean of St Paul's. To the right is Paul Mount's

Amicale

The Blitz

The German word for lightning, 'Blitz' was used by the British press to describe the German bombing offensive against Britain in 1940 and 1941. This concentrated, direct bombing of industrial targets and civilian centres began with heavy raids on London from 7th September 1940 to 11th May 1941. This overlaps the period that became known as the Battle of Britain, which officially lasted from 10th July to 31th October 1940. Hitler and Hermann Goering's plans to destroy the Royal Air Force ahead of an invasion of Britain were failing, so they changed their tactics to the sustained bombing of civilian targets. It's estimated that 32,000 civilians were killed and 87,000 seriously injured during the Blitz, which destroyed two million houses – 60 per cent of which were in London.

2007 abstract stainless-steel sculpture, **Amicale** ⓰ . At the western end of the Festival Gardens is a wall fountain, at the rear of which is Austrian Georg Ehrlich's lovely bronze, **The Young Lovers** ⓱ , installed in 1973.

The Young Lovers

From Festival Gardens, cross New Change to Watling Street and at the northern edge of the small garden in front of 25 Cannon Street is a bust of **Vice-Admiral**

Walk 7

Arthur Phillip ⑱ (1738-1814), a resin copy of Charles Leonard Hartwell's original 1932 monument which was destroyed in the Blitz. Admiral Phillip was commander of the 'first fleet' that arrived in Botany Bay (Australia) in 1788 and was also the first governor of New South Wales and the founder of Sydney. Cross to the south of Cannon Street and on the right, just past Distaff Lane, is Bracken House (Grade II* listed) – a late example of modern Classicism – which has an interesting **Zodiac Clock** ⑲ above the entrance designed

by Frank Dobson. The clock has Winston Churchill's face at the centre of a golden sunburst, surrounded by gilded signs of the zodiac on an azure background.

Walk back along Cannon Street towards St Paul's and on the left – opposite Festival

St Lawrence Fountain

Gardens – sits the **St Lawrence & Mary Magdalene Drinking Fountain** ⑳ , designed by John Robinson with bronze sculpture by Joseph Durham. Originally installed in 1866 outside the Church of St Lawrence Jewry, it was dismantled in the '70s and installed here in 2010. Walk along Old Change Court (behind the fountain) to see Michael Ayrton's **Icarus** ㉑ , unveiled in 1973. Much of Ayrton's work was centred on the myth of Daedalus and his son Icarus, who attempted to escape from Crete on wings that Daedalus constructed from feathers and wax; Icarus ignored his father's instructions not to fly too close to the sun and his wings melted, causing him to fall into the sea and drown. Carry on down Old Change Court to Distaff Lane, and turn left to St Nicholas Cole Abbey. The Grade I listed abbey was rebuilt in 1672-8 by Sir Christopher Wren, with soaring stone columns and lovely stained glass windows, and provides a rare tranquil oasis in

St Bride's

St Bride's has a history going back as far as the 7th century – the current church is the eighth to stand on this site. It was built by Sir Christopher Wren from 1672 to replace the 11th-century Norman church destroyed in the Great Fire in 1666. Grade I listed, it has Wren's tallest spire (226ft/21m), designed in a series of tiers – and is said to have inspired the shape of modern wedding cakes. As befits its location in Fleet Street, St Bride's has a long association with men of letters (notably the press), and has been dubbed the spiritual home of printing and the media.

Food & Drink

22 The Wren: Atmospheric café in St Nicholas Cole Abbey serving breakfast, lunch and outstanding coffee (Mon-Fri 7am-4.30pm, closed weekends, £).

32 Ye Olde Cheshire Cheese: Grade II listed and renowned for its literary associations – Charles Dickins and Mark Twain drank here – the Cheese is one of London's oldest hostelries. Today, it offers Sam Smith's well-priced ales and traditional pub fare (11.30am-11pm, closed Sunday, £).

49 Fernandez & Wells: Located in Somerset House, this café-bar is a good choice for coffee and cake or tapas and an early evening drink (8/9am-10/11pm, 6pm Sundays, £).

National Firefighters Memorial

depicting three firefighters in action during the Second World War. It was unveiled in 1991 and commemorates the lives of all firefighters lost in the line of duty. From the memorial continue west along Carter Lane, and go right on Dean's Court and then left on St Paul's Churchyard to reach Ludgate Hill. Walk down to Ludgate Circus, where in the northwest corner, is Ludgate House and Francis William Doyle-Jones' (1934) memorial to writer and journalist **Edgar Wallace 24** (1875-1932). The inscription on the bronze plaque reads: 'He knew wealth and poverty, yet had walked with kings and kept his bearing. Of his talents he gave lavishly to authorship, but to Fleet Street he gave his heart.' Cross Fleet Street and take the second left down St Bride's Avenue to visit **St Bride's 25** (see box opposite).

Return to Fleet Street and turn left, where a few steps along above the door of number 85, is William Reid Dick's 1939 bronze **The Herald 26** . Take the next left down Salisbury Court, where a short way down on the left is a blue plaque to diarist **Samuel Pepys 27** , who was born

The Herald

the City. It also houses a tranquil café called **The Wren 22** .

Retrace your steps along Distaff Lane heading west and at the end go right on Sermon Lane to the junction with Carter Lane. On the left-hand corner is John William Mills' **National Firefighters Memorial 23** , a lively bronze in a house on this site in 1633 (not 1632 as shown on the plaque!). Continue to Salisbury Square to see the **Robert Waithman Memorial** 28 , an obelisk in the centre of a small garden. Waithman (1764-1833) was an MP, Sheriff and Lord Mayor of London and the memorial is inscribed, 'The friend of liberty in evil times'. Leave the square on the eastern side, where it becomes Dorset Rise and a short way along on the left, just opposite Hutton Street, is Michael Sandle's

St George & the Dragon

striking modern sculpture of **St George & the Dragon** 29 . The life-size bronze unveiled in 1988 depicts St George dressed in armour standing in his stirrups with a lance in his hands, which he has thrust into the dragon that's below the tilting grid and wrapped around the supporting framework. Four shaped tubes extend to form the dragon's mouth, ending in nozzles that create a fountain.

Retrace your steps to Fleet Street and turn left, where by the door of number 72-78 (Chronicle House) is a bust of **T. P. O'Connor** (1848-1929), journalist and parliamentarian, by Doyle-Jones (1936). The inscription reads: 'His pen could lay bare the bones of a book or the soul of a statesman in a few vivid lines.' Cross over to **Mary Queen of Scots House** 31 (number 143-4, now a Pret a Manger outlet), where there's a statue of Mary Stuart (1542-1587) in a niche above the entrance on the first floor. It was a romantic idea of the developer Sir John Tollemache MP, who was an admirer of Mary, beheaded in 1587 for plotting to assassinate Elizabeth I. Next door at number 145 (down an alleyway) is **Ye Olde Cheshire Cheese 32** , one of London's oldest and most

---

Temple Bar Memorial

The original Temple Bar (see page 85) was a barrier to regulate trade into the City. It was the custom for the monarch to halt here before entering the City of London, to allow the Lord Mayor to offer the Corporation's pearl-encrusted Sword of State as a token of loyalty. The name Temple Bar was commonly used to refer to Sir Christopher Wren's 17th-century arch, which spanned the road until being removed in 1878 (it's now in Paternoster Square). Following its removal, Horace Jones designed a memorial to mark Temple Bar, unveiled in 1880. The elaborate pedestal in New Renaissance style serves as the base for a sculpture by Charles Bell Birch commonly called the Griffin, although it's actually a dragon (in reference to the heraldic crest of the Corporation of the City of London). The pedestal is decorated with Joseph Boehm's statues of Queen Victoria and Edward VII.

St Paul's to the Strand

tmospheric taverns, rebuilt a year fter the 1666 Great Fire.

Keep heading west along Fleet Street and just past Fetter Lane on

the right is **St Dunstan-in-the-West** 33 . There has been a church here for many centuries, although the current one was built between 1830 and 1833.

King Lud & Sons

It's best known for its clock which was the first public clock in London to have a minute hand. It was made by Thomas Harris in 1671 for the old medieval church. When the building was demolished in the early 19th century, the clock was saved and was returned to the current church in 1935. In a recess behind the clock either side of a pair of bells are two 'giant' figures – perhaps representing Gog and Magog – which turn their heads and strike the hours and quarters. Below the clock is Alfred Charles William Harmsworth's memorial bust of **Lord Northcliffe** 34 (1865-1922), a British newspaper and publishing magnate who arranged for the return of the clock.

The courtyard to the right contains statues of **King Lud & Sons** 35 . Lud was a mythical

sovereign from pre-Roman times who, it's said, founded London. Also here is a statue of **Queen Elizabeth I** 36 (1533-1603) which dates from 1586 and is the only one known to have been made during her reign; it was originally installed on the Ludgate, one of the gated entrances to the City – and the burial place of the aforementioned King Lud. Continue along Fleet Street and cross Chancery Lane to number 193 on the right-hand corner and look up to see Giuseppe Grandi's marble statue of **Kaled** 37 , aka Lara's Page. A woman dressed as a page boy, Kaled is a figure from Lord Byron's poem *Lara*, a tale of disguises and tragic love. Some 50m further on in the middle of the road – in front of the Royal Courts of Justice – is the **Temple Bar Memorial** 38 (see box opposite), surmounted by a magnificent bronze dragon by Charles Bell Birch.

Royal Courts of Justice

A few steps past the memorial are the main gates to the **Royal Courts of Justice** 39 (aka the Law Courts, Grade I listed), where there are two elaborate carved porches fitted with iron gates. The carvings over the outer porch consist of heads of the country's

St Clement Danes

This beautiful church sits isolated on an island in the middle of the Strand. There has been a place of worship here for over 1,000 years; the original church was reputedly built by Danes expelled from the City of London by King Alfred in the 9th century, and named after St Clement, patron saint of mariners. It's mentioned in the *Domesday Book* (1086) and was in the care of the Knights Templar from 1170 to 1312. St Clement Danes escaped damage in the Great Fire of 1666 but was rebuilt in 1680-2 by Sir Christopher Wren; the west tower was added by Joshua Marshall in 1669 and the familiar spire by James Gibbs in 1720. In 1953, the church was donated to the Air Council and rebuilt after a worldwide appeal; it was re-consecrated in 1958 as the Central Church of the Royal Air Force. Today, it's a shrine dedicated to all those of the Allied Air Forces who gave their lives during the Second World War.

the last great wonders of Victorian neo-Gothic revival architecture. The finished building contained 35 million Portland stone bricks, over 3.5mi (5.6km) of corridors and some 1,000 clocks, many of which had to be wound by hand.

Just past the Law Courts, at the eastern end of **St Clement Danes** (see box), is Percy Fitzgerald's (1910) statue of polymath **Samuel Johnson** ㊶ (1709-1784) – essayist, philologist, biographer, wit, poet, moralist, dramatist, political writer, talker and critic (etc.). There are three large bronze reliefs around the pedestal; on the front is a profile of Johnson's biographer James Boswell, on the left-hand side is Johnson with Mrs Hester Thrale (diarist and author), while on right-hand side is Johnson with Boswell in the Highlands.

Samuel Johnson

In front of Clement Danes is Faith Winter's statue of Air Chief Marshal **Lord Dowding** ㊷ (1882-1970), and Marshal of the RAF **Sir Arthur Harris** ㊸ (1892-1984) by T. Hart and Michael Goss. Dowding was commander of RAF Fighter Command during the

most eminent judges and lawyers at the time the building was constructed (it officially opened in 1882). Over the highest point of the upper arch is a figure of Jesus, lower down (to the left and right) are figures of Solomon and Alfred the Great, while Moses is at the northern front of the building. Also at the northern front, over the Judges' entrance, are a stone cat and dog, representing litigants fighting in court. Designed by George Edmund Street and built in the 1870s, the building is one of

St Paul's to the Strand

attle of Britain and is generally credited with playing a crucial role in Britain's defence. Arthur 'Bomber' Harris, on the other hand, is a controversial figure – as Commander in Chief 1942-1945 of RAF Bomber Command, he was responsible for the widespread bombing of German cities during the war. His statue was unveiled in 1992 on the 50th anniversary of the first Allied 1,000 bomber raid on 30th May/31st May 1942.

Just past Clement Danes, opposite Australia House, is Hamo Thorneycroft's (1905) impressive bronze of **William Gladstone** 44 (1809-1898). At each corner of the monument there are allegorical groups representing (clockwise from the front) brotherhood, aspiration, courage and education. Gladstone was the Liberal Party leader who served for 12 years as Prime Minister over four terms, from 1868 to 1894. He was one of Britain's most formidable politicians, as this imposing monument vividly illustrates.

On the other side of Aldwych is Australia House, the longest continuously occupied foreign mission in London, officially opened in 1918. The building boasts numerous statues and monuments, including Australian Sir Edgar Bertram Mackennal's striking **Phoebus Driving the Horses of the Sun** 45 .

Continue around Aldwych to the Aldwych Theatre, where outside India House opposite (in India Place) is a bust of **Jawaharlal 'Pandit' Nehru** 46 (1889-1964), the first Prime Minister of India. He was a central figure in Indian

William Gladstone

politics, and ruled India from its establishment as an independent nation in 1947 until his death. In April 2009, the statue was beheaded, allegedly by protestors from a Tamil Tigers demonstration. India House itself is adorned with a number of sculptures and decorative plaques representing the Indian states. Return to the Strand, where opposite India House is **Somerset House** 47 (see box, page 94).

In the quadrangle of Somerset House is John Bacon's (1789) statue of **George III** 48 (1738-1820), who reigned from 1760 to 1820. The statue is formally titled 'George III and the River Thames' and depicts the king

'Pandit' Nehru

Walk 7

> ## Somerset House
>
> A large Neoclassical building designed by Sir William Chambers in 1776 and the former home of the Royal Academy of Arts, Somerset House is now a centre for the visual arts and hosts open-air concerts, film screenings and art exhibitions. It also houses the splendid Courtauld Gallery, which has a gem of an art collection, ranging from early Renaissance to 20th-century modernist works. During the summer months, 55 fountains dance in the magnificent courtyard, while in winter it's transformed into one of London's favourite ice rinks.

Peter II, Count of Savoy

dressed in Roman apparel and leaning on a rudder, flanked by the prow of a Roman boat and a lion, while Father Thames reclines on a lower, semi-circular plinth. Within Somerset House there are a number of excellent cafés, restaurants and bars, including **Fernandez & Wells** 49.

Continue along the Strand, passing two of London's most illustrious hotels: the Strand Palace built in 1909 and the Savoy (1889); the latter was built by the impresario Richard D'Oyly Carte with the profits made from staging Gilbert and Sullivan productions. Above the Savoy's entrance is Frank Lynn-Jenkins' 1904 statue of **Peter II, Count of Savoy** 50 (1203-1268), from

George III

whom the hotel takes its name. Peter wasn't a count when he came to London in the 1240s (he inherited the title in 1263); he was, however, the uncle of Eleanor of Provence, who had just married Henry III. Henry made him Earl of Richmond and gave him the site on the north bank of the Thames where he built the Savoy Palace, the grandest townhouse in medieval London.

Zimbabwe House

A few metres further along, on the north side of the Strand, is **Zimbabwe House** 51, home of the Zimbabwean Embassy. Designed in 1907-8 by Charles Holden (1875-1960) to be the HQ of the British Medical Association, its façade has caused controversy for over a century, due to the installation of 18 larger-than-life nude figures by Jacob Epstein in 1908, then regarded by many as far too graphic. The male and female figures symbolise the Ages of Man, although they take inspiration from classical Indian rt rather than European tradition. When the Rhodesian government ook over the building in 1923, a iece of masonry fell off one of he statues onto the street below, hich was used as a convenient excuse to chisel away all the statues' extremities (including, of course, the 'rude' bits), which is vhy today they're oddly defaced.

From here, it's a short hop to he south side of the Strand and Charing Cross station, which narks the end of the walk.

Somerset House, winter

Somerset House, summer

1. Venus Fountain
2. My Children
3. Saatchi Gallery
4. The Gallery Mess
5. Sir Hans Sloane
6. Royal Hospital, Chelsea
7. Chelsea Pensioner
8. Charles II
9. Chillianwalla Monument
10. Carabiniers Memorial
11. Chelsea Physic Garden
12. Sir Hans Sloane (cast)
13. Rossetti Drinking Fountain
14. The Boy David
15. Lamp Standard
16. Albert Bridge
17. Boy with a Dolphin
18. Atalanta
19. Thomas Carlyle
20. George Sparkes
21. Sir Thomas More
22. Chelsea Old Church
23. The Awakening
24. Female Lower Torso
25. Crosby Hall
26. James McNeill Whistler
27. Peace Pagoda
28. Australian Memorial Garden
29. ANZAC Boulder
30. XXIV Division Memorial
31. Pump House Gallery
32. Three Standing Figures
33. Single Form
34. Pear Tree Café
35. Mason's Arms

● Places of Interest   Food & Drink

Sloane Square to Battersea Park

WALK 8

Distance: 4½ miles (7¼ km)
Terrain: easy
Duration: 2-3 hours
Start: Sloane Square tube
End: Battersea Park rail
Postcode: SW1W 8BB

SLOANE SQUARE TO BATTERSEA PARK

This walk starts in Sloane Square, in the Royal Borough of Chelsea & Kensington, one of London's most affluent and fashionable districts. Sloane Square forms the boundary between the two largest aristocratic estates in London, the Grosvenor and Cadogan Estates, and is named after its former owner Sir Hans Sloane – the area was once known as 'Hans Town' – whose private collection was the foundation of the British Museum.

Hans Sloane

From here, we visit Duke of York Square and the Saatchi Gallery before heading south to the magnificent Royal Hospital, Chelsea and taking a walk along the Chelsea Embankment. The Embankment has long been a popular venue for public works of art and a number commemorate former residents, particularly along Cheyne Walk, which was home to artists such as Holbein, Turner, Whistler and Dante Gabriel Rossetti, and writers such as Tobias Smollett, Henry James and Ian Fleming. A stylish street with a long history, Cheyne Walk takes its name from William Lord Cheyne (1657-1728), who owned the manor of Chelsea until 1712, when it was sold to Sir Hans Sloane.

From Cheyne Walk we cross Albert Bridge – opened in 1873 and one of London's most attractive bridges – to visit Battersea Park, a public park opened in 1858 by Queen Victoria. Covering 200 acres (83ha), Battersea is one of London's largest and most interesting green spaces and houses many fine works of art, including a number of moving war memorials. In contrast it also has the striking Peace Pagoda overlooking the Thames.

Start Walking…

Exit Sloane Square tube station and cross Holbein Place to the square, which was laid out in 1771 to a plan by Henry Holland and son. In the centre is Gilbert Ledward's fine **Venus Fountain** ❶ , installed in 1953, portraying a kneeling nude Venus, while the fountain pedestal contains a relief depicting Charles II and Nell Gwyn by the Thames. The square also contains a First World War memorial by Sir Reginald Blomfield (1920) in the shape of a Portland stone cross.

From Sloane Square, head west along King's Road. Opposite Cadogan Gardens (at the rear of Peter Jones store) on the left-hand side is a passageway, part of Duke of York Square, where you see Allister Bowtell's two bronze sculptures, **My Children** ❷ .

Royal Hospital, Chelsea

Founded in 1682 by Charles II for veteran soldiers and designed by Sir Christopher Wren, the Royal Hospital is built around three courtyards; the central courtyard opens to the south, with side courtyards to the east and west. The building remains almost unchanged from Wren's original, except for minor alterations by Robert Adam between 1765 and 1782, and the stables which were added by Sir John Soane in 1814. Today, the hospital is home to some 400 Chelsea pensioners, who receive free board, lodging, nursing care and a distinctive red uniform. Much of the site is open to visitors, including the great hall, octagon, chapel, courtyards and grounds. There's also a small museum dedicated to the hospital's history. (See www.chelsea-pensioners.co.uk for more information.)

The figures represent orphaned children – one seated and the other vaulting a post – from the former Royal Military Asylum. In 1801, Duke of York Square was home to a school for military orphans, which later became a military school and barracks; it was acquired by Cadogan Estates in 1998 and redeveloped into an award-winning shopping and dining destination. Continue along the passageway and go right to

Royal Hospital, Chelsea

where the square opens out. On the left is the **Saatchi Gallery** ❸, founded by Charles Saatchi in 1985, which relocated to the Duke of York's HQ in 2008. It's one of London's major contemporary art galleries, attracting over 1½ million visitors a year, and features an excellent (if expensive) café, the **Gallery Mess** ❹, should you need a caffeine boost to get you on your way.

Saatchi Gallery

On the right, facing the Saatchi Gallery is Simon Smith's statue of **Sir Hans Sloane** ❺ (1660–1753), dressed in full wig and academic robes, unveiled in 2007. It's a copy of John Michael Rysbrack's original alabaster work of 1737,

which was previously in the Physic Garden (see box below) and is now in the British Museum. Sloane purchased the manor of Chelsea in 1712 and provided the grounds for the Chelsea Physic Garden. Return to King's Road and go left down Cheltenham Terrace (behind Partridges food store) and bear left at the end onto Franklins Row, which leads to Royal Hospital Road. Opposite is the entrance to Sir Christopher Wren's **Royal Hospital, Chelsea** ❻ (see box, page 99), one of London's most elegant and historic buildings.

As you explore the hospital grounds, there are some interesting memorials. On the north front of the building, facing Royal Hospital Road, is Philip Jackson's statue of a **Chelsea Pensioner** ❼, unveiled in 2000 to commemorate the Millennium. Around the base is the soldiers' prayer, based on that said by Sir Jacob Astley (1579-1652) before the Battle of Edgehill in 1642: 'O Lord, thou knowest how busy I must be this day. If I forget Thee, do not forget me'. In the central Figure Court is a celebrated statue of **Charles II** ❽

Charles II

Chelsea Physic Garden

The 3½ acre (1.4ha) garden is a living museum, as well as a haven of beauty and relaxation. It was founded in 1673 and is London's oldest botanical garden – and Britain's second-oldest after the one at Oxford University which dates back to 1621. However, unlike most other London gardens, there's a hefty entrance fee (which varies by season) that must also be paid to access the nice café, Tangerine Dream. The entrance is in Swan Walk.

Sloane Square to Battersea Park

1630-1685) by Grinling Gibbons, the greatest wood carver and sculptor of his day. The 7ft 6in (2.3m) statue was cast in copper alloy and was originally gilded; it was bronzed in 1782 but was re-gilded in 2002 to celebrate Elizabeth II's Golden Jubilee. It portrays the king as a Roman general, holding a baton as a sign of his imperial authority. Next to the flagpole in the Figure Court is the Singora Cannon, made in Singora (modern Songkhla in southern Thailand) around 1623, bearing the seal of Sultan Sulaiman Shah; it was captured by the British during the third Anglo-Burmese War (1885-1887).

In the centre of the hospital's Ranelagh Gardens is the **Chillianwalla Monument** ❾ in memory of the 255 soldiers of the 24th Regiment of the British East India Company who fell at Chillianwalla (in the Punjab, now part of Pakistan) in January 1849. The monument, a tall square obelisk inscribed with the names of the dead, is surmounted by a crown and gold painted globe. In the southeast corner of the gardens (opposite Chelsea Bridge) is Adrian Jones' 1905 **Carabiniers Memorial** ❿ (Sixth Dragoon Guards), which commemorates the fallen in the Boer Wars in South Africa. From Ranelagh Gardens head west along Chelsea Embankment, where around 600m along is the **Chelsea Physic Garden** ⓫ (see box opposite). A statue of **Sir Hans Sloane** ⓬ stands here, although, like the one in Duke of York Square, it's a copy of Rysbrack's original.

Albert Bridge

Designed by Rowland Mason Ordish and opened in 1873, Albert Bridge was originally a toll bridge; the tolls were unsuccessful and were scrapped after six years, although the tollbooths remain in place and are the only surviving examples in London. The bridge was nicknamed 'The Trembling Lady' due to its tendency to vibrate when large numbers of people walked over it – signs at the entrances warn 'troops must break step when marching over this bridge'. It looks particularly stunning when illuminated at night.

Just over Royal Hospital Road from the Physic Garden is the start of Cheyne Walk and, in front, Chelsea Embankment Gardens, where there's an abundance of memorials and sculptures. Look for Ford Madox Brown's **Rossetti Drinking Fountain** ⓭ , which stands opposite 16 Cheyne Walk where Dante Gabriel Rossetti (1828-1882) lived for 20 years. Rossetti was a British poet and painter who founded the Pre-Raphaelite Brotherhood in 1848, along with William Holman Hunt and John Everett Millais. Around 50m further on, just

Boy David

Walk 8

before the end of the first garden section, is **The Boy David** ⑭, a fibreglass sculpture by Edward Bainbridge Copnall. The original Boy David bronze by Francis Derwent Wood was the model for the Machine Gun Corps memorial at Hyde Park Corner; it was presented to the Borough of Chelsea in 1963 but was later stolen.

Boy with Dolphin

Cross to the south side of the Embankment, where just before Albert Bridge is an ornamental green-painted, cast-iron **Lamp Standard** ⑮ made by Coalbrookdale (there's another near Chelsea Old Church – see below), which commemorates the opening of Chelsea Embankment in 1874. It features two young boys climbing the lamp – the lower boy handing up a burning torch to light the lamp – while below, two elongated conch shells spew forth cornucopias of fruit. Cross back to the north side of the Embankment and over Oakley Street, opposite **Albert Bridge** ⑯ (see box, page 101), where

on the corner is David Wynne's graceful bronze **Boy with a Dolphin** ⑰, unveiled in 1975; the boy was modelled on the artist's son, Roland, who tragically died at the age of 35, and the statue is dedicated to him. Back on the riverside opposite is a green Cabmen's Shelter, Grade II listed and one of just a dozen remaining in London, offering rest and refreshments to black cab drivers. Just past the shelter is **Atalanta** ⑱ – a swift-footed huntress in Greek mythology – a beautiful bronze nude by Francis Derwent Wood (1929).

In the middle of the next section of Chelsea Embankment Gardens – in front of Cheyne Row – is Sir Joseph Edgar Boehm's (1881) statue of **Thomas Carlyle** ⑲ (1795-1881), historian, philosopher and satirist. Thomas and Jane Carlyle, a celebrated literary couple of their day, lived at number 24 Cheyne Row, one of London's most original early 18th-century streets. Their home, a beautiful Queen Anne property from 1708, is open to the public (Wed-Sun 11am-5pm, entrance fee) and provides a fascinating insight in to what life was like in the home of an educated middle-class Victorian couple.

Around 50m further on, just past where Cheyne Walk meets the main thoroughfare along the Thames Embankment, is a memorial by Charles Barry Jr (1880) to **George Sparkes** ⑳

The Awakening

Sloane Square to Battersea Park

Food & Drink

(4) Gallery Mess: The Saatchi Gallery's café-restaurant has all-day eating, an elegant ambience and a sunny terrace (10am-11.30pm, Sun 10am-7pm, ££).

(34) Pear Tree Café: Delicious dishes using seasonal produce, which you can enjoy while watching the ducks and boats on Battersea Park's boating lake (Mon 8am-6pm, Tue-Sat 8am-10pm, Sun 8am-8pm, £).

(35) Mason's Arms: A Fuller's gastropub serving British favourites with a French twist (noon-11pm, Sat 10.30am-11pm, Sun until 10.30pm, £).

(1810-1878) of the East India Company, in the form of a drinking fountain with four dog troughs. Between the fountain and Chelsea Old Church is Leslie Cubitt Bevis' (1969) garish seated bronze of **Sir Thomas More** (21) (1478-1535), with black robes and golden face and hands. More was a philosopher, theologian and statesman (Lord Chancellor) under Henry VIII – a risky business! He opposed Henry's Reformation and paid the price by losing his head.

Chelsea Old Church (22) was the parish church of Chelsea when it was a village, and parts of the building date from 1157. The handsome church is the only one in London to retain a chained library (albeit a small one), a curious throwback to medieval times, and it also boasts London's second-finest collection of church monuments after Westminster Abbey.

Continuing west, just past Old Church Street is Ropers Gardens, a small sunken garden with a fine nude statue, **The Awakening** (23), an early work by celebrated sculptor Gilbert Ledward (1915) who was born in Chelsea. Also in the gardens is Sir Jacob Epstein's unfinished stone relief of a **Female Lower Torso** (24), which stands on the site of a studio where he worked from 1909-1914. The fragment was set by Stephen Gardiner and unveiled by Sir Caspar John in the '70s. Next, cross Danvers Street to red-brick **Crosby Hall** (25), the surviving part of a Bishopsgate mansion built in 1466-75 for Sir John Crosby, a wealthy wool merchant. What makes it really remarkable is that the building was moved stone-by-stone from Bishopsgate to Chelsea in 1910 to save it from demolition. A little further on, in the gardens just past Battersea Bridge, is Nicholas Dimbleby's 2005 statue of

Whistler

Walk 8

James McNeill Whistler 26 (1834-1903). Whistler was an American artist active during the American Gilded Age, who was based primarily in the UK (he lived at 96 Cheyne Walk).

Retrace your steps along the Embankment to Albert Bridge and cross to the south side of the Thames to Battersea Park, which contains a number of memorials and statues. Take the first entrance to the park, on the left just past the bridge, and walk along the northern edge parallel with the river to the striking **Peace Pagoda** 27 (see box), installed in 1985. Continue along the riverside path for another 250m and turn right before the car park; cross over Carriage Drive North and follow Carriage Drive East past Thrive Battersea's main garden on the left. Just past the garden turn right and then left to the **Australian Memorial Garden** 28 , where there's a memorial,

erected in 1995, to the 5,397 Australian air crew who were lost in action over Europe during the Second World War. Located nearby is the **ANZAC Boulder** 29 (unveiled in 2000), an Australian sandstone rock mounted with a bronze plaque by Ray Ewers incorporating a relief map of the Gallipoli peninsula, where thousands of Australians died in the First World War.

XXIV Division Memorial

A short distance from the Australian Memorial, on the other side of the path, is the striking **XXIV Division Memorial** 30 by Eric Henri Kennington (1924), who had served in two battalions of the London Regiment and undertook the commission for free, even buying the stone himself. It commemorates the 24th East Surrey Infantry Division, which served on the Western Front in the First World War, where it suffered the loss of over 35,000 men killed, wounded or missing. The memorial depicts three infantry soldiers – one modelled on the poet and writer Robert Graves (who served with the 3rd Battalion, Royal Welch Fusiliers) – with helmets, rifles and full kit, and a serpent at their feet, standing upon a three part columnar base.

From the XXIV Division Memorial head south, cross over Central Avenue and take the path

---

Peace Pagoda

A gift to London from the Nipponzan Myōhōji Order of Japanese Buddhist monks, the striking pagoda is regarded by the Buddhist order (which maintains it) as a spiritual centre for London. Made of Portland stone and wood, the pagoda is 110ft (33.5m) high and includes four gilded statues of the Buddha – facing north, south, east and west – making various *mudras* (hand gestures) with different symbolic meanings.

Pump House Gallery

Housed in a four-storey water tower (Grade II listed) built in 1861 to supply water to the lake and cascades, the gallery opened in 1999 and hosts a year-round programme of contemporary art exhibitions.

towards the handsome Italianate **Pump House Gallery** ❸❶ (free, Wed-Sun, 11am-5pm, see box). From the gallery follow the path west around the top of the Ladies Pond, where after around 150m you come to another of the park's impressive sculptures, Henry Moore's **Three Standing Figures** ❸❷. The 7ft (2.1m) stone statue – depicting three women draped in flowing garments – was created in 1947 and has stood in the park since 1950.

Continue along the wooded path around the western end of the lake – passing the sub-tropical gardens on the right, which contain some majestic oak, ash and palm trees – to the south of the lake. Around half way along the southern edge is Barbara Hepworth's (1964) statue **Single Form** ❸❸, a huge bronze over 10ft (3m) high. A typical Hepworth 'bottle-opener', it's a copy of her memorial to her friend Dag Hammarskjold, the UN Secretary General who died in a plane crash in 1961, and was

erected here in 1964; the original stands outside the UN Building in New York. The path continues around the lake to the park's main entrance on Carriage Drive South. A short distance further round, at the eastern end of the lake, is the **Pear Tree Café** **34**, a popular spot for alfresco dining.

Exit to Queen's Circus, walk around it anti-clockwise to Queenstown Road and go left on Battersea Park Road at the end to Battersea Park railway station – and the end of the walk. If you're peckish there are a number of options close by, including the **Mason's Arms** **35** opposite the station.

Single Form

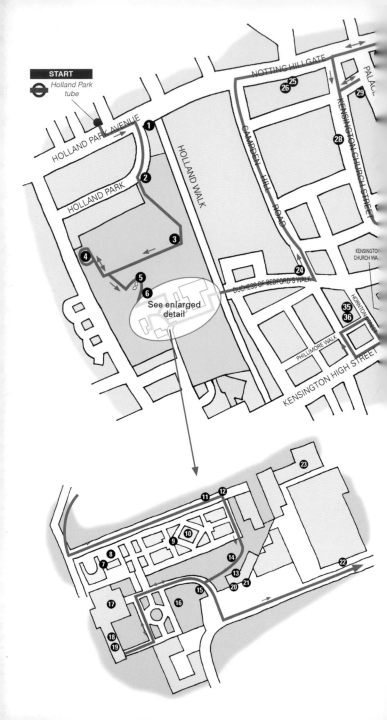

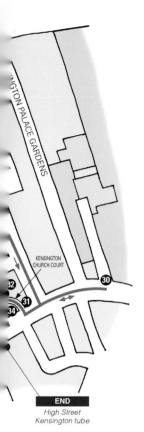

KENSINGTON PALACE GARDENS

KENSINGTON CHURCH COURT

END
High Street Kensington tube

● Places of Interest   Food & Drink

WALK 9

Holland Park to High St Kensington

Distance: 3½ miles (5½ km)
Terrain: easy
Duration: 2-3 hours
Start: Holland Park tube
End: High Street Kensington tube
Postcode: W11 3RB

From Holland Park to High Street Kensington, this walk wanders through some of London's most exclusive streets and glorious green spaces. Named after the 3rd Baron Holland, Holland Park is one of London's most affluent districts, known for its attractive large Victorian townhouses. And at its heart, covering some 54 acres (22ha), is the Borough of Kensington and Chelsea's largest park.

Kyoto Garden

The first half of the walk concentrates on Holland Park itself – one of London's most attractive and romantic spots and home to a glorious assemblage of monuments and sculpture, as well as tranquil oases such as Kyoto Garden. From Holland Park we head east and north to the fringes of Notting Hill, a cosmopolitan neighbourhood that hosts the annual Carnival and which – since being developed in the 1820s – has been associated with artists and 'counter' culture.

From Notting Hill Gate we go south along 'eccentrically posh' Kensington Church Street, an old part of town renowned for its upmarket art and antiques shops. The walk culminates in Kensington High Street, which has a number of important buildings, such as the Design Museum, and is home to the UK offices of major record labels such as Sony Music and EMI, although most people visit for the retail therapy opportunities!

Holland Park to High St Kensington

Start Walking...

From Holland Park tube station, cross to the south side of Holland Park Avenue and go left to walk to Holland Park (the road) where, on the opposite corner, is one of London's most bizarre statues: **St Volodymyr ❶**, ruler of Ukraine from 980 to 1015. Volodymyr established Christianity in Ukraine in 988 and the statue was erected by Ukrainians in the UK to celebrate the 1,000th anniversary in 1988. Turn down Holland Park and enter the park via the **Sun Trap Entrance ❷** – an archway in a white wall on the left – which leads to the Sun Terrace. Go straight ahead and take the second path on the right, which takes you to George Frederic Watts' superb statue of **Henry Richard Vassall-Fox ❸**, who's seated on a throne-like chair in the middle of a pond in woodland. The 3rd Baron Holland (1773-1840) was a major figure in Whig politics in the early 19th century and he was Lord Privy Seal 1806-1807 in the 'Ministry of All the Talents' coalition government.

From the statue take the path leading to the western side of the park and go right at the end to the small garden in the northwest corner by the Abbotsbury Road entrance. Here is Wendy Taylor's

imposing bronze sculpture, **Tortoises with Triangle and Time ❹**, an imaginative sundial. Installed in 2000 to celebrate the new millennium, it consists of two giant tortoises, one of which is supporting a sundial needle on its back. From here, walk south and follow the diagonal path leading to the magical Japanese **Kyoto Garden ❺** (see box) with its waterfall and pond. There are actually two Japanese gardens close together. The adjoining Fukushima Garden was opened in 2012 to commemorate the support of the British people following the Fukushima nuclear disaster resulting from the March 2011 tsunami.

From Kyoto Garden take the path south, and you'll pass Sean Henry's polychrome sculpture **Walking Man ❻** (2000) on the left. At first glance 'he' appears

Tortoises with Triangle & Time

109

Walk 9

Milo of Croton

to be a fellow walker, but Henry's bronze painted figure is larger than life, like a three-dimensional painting.

Just past the sculpture you enter the **Napoleon Garden** ❼ , which takes its name from a bust of Napoleon by the Venetian sculptor Canova that used to be located here. It's a discreet corner of the park which has been used to showcase contemporary sculpture since the 19th century. Continue to the left where there's a small area with a giant chess set, followed by the Sundial Garden with an **Armillary Sphere** ❽ at its centre. Armillary spheres are thought to have been developed by the Greek astronomer and philosopher Ptolemy in the 2nd century AD. They comprise a number of rings, called *armillae* in Latin, representing the major circles on the celestial sphere, such as the horizon and the celestial equator. The Holland Park sphere is a

sundial; on the inside of the equator circle are etched the hours of the day and the time is shown by the shadow cast by the north pole/south pole axis rod (the gnomon), which points due north.

From the Sundial Garden you enter the magnificent **Dutch Garden** ❾ , with vibrant flowerbeds enclosed by box hedges and numerous benches dedicated to departed loved ones. In the centre of the garden is a 19th-century bronze, **Milo of Croton** ❿ (inscription on the ground). Milo was a legendary 6th-century BC Olympic athlete who hailed from Croton, a Greek settlement in southern Italy. On the northern wall is the limestone **Ancient Melancholy Man** ⓫ secreted in a corner of the old brick wall – believed to date from the 1500s – and in the northeast corner is a **Dutch Wall Trough** ⓬ , one of the house's original fountains; it's inscribed with the

Dutch Garden

Holland Park to High St Kensington

words: 'Earth would be less fair without trees to grace her valleys, Hide her scars, cast cool shade, In gardens here.'

Leave the Dutch Garden via the southeast corner, passing the **Holland Park Café** 13 on your left. A little further along on the right of the path is John Macallan Swan's 1902 bronze sculpture of a **Boy with Bear Cubs** 14 . This delightful work depicts a naked boy standing on a rock with a bowl balanced on his left hip, turning round to view one bear climbing up, and in doing so tipping his bowl of tit-bits to one side where the second bear rears up for an opportune snack. Follow the path around to the left, just past the archway, where the building on the left is the original **Ice House** 15 , now used as an art gallery with an annual programme of exhibitions from April to September. In front of the Ice House in the Iris Garden is William Pye's 1999 fountain **Sibirica** 16 , based on a species of iris. Beyond the fountain is the romantic **Belvedere Restaurant** 17 , housed in what was the summer ballroom. In front of the restaurant is a rose garden and to its left is the **Orangery** 18 , an elegant building flooded with natural light – this is where Lord and Lady Holland held their many receptions. Inside the Orangery

are two 19th-century male nude bronzes, the **Wrestlers of Herculaneum** 19 (sculptor unknown), copies of 4th-century statues that came from the ancient city, destroyed in 79AD by an eruption from nearby Mt Vesuvius in southern Italy.

Retrace your steps to the entrance archway by the café, where there are two more fine sculptures, displayed indoors to protect them from inclement weather: Eric Gill's **The Maid** 20 and Sir Jacob Epstein's **The Sun God** 21 , a 6ft (1.8m) relief of a male figure carved in limestone. From the café go left, where a short distance along are the magnificent Portland stone **Gate Piers** 22 in front of the terrace. Commissioned by Inigo Jones and

Holland House

Cope Castle (as it was then known) was built between 1604 and 1607 for Sir Walter Cope (1553-1614), Chancellor to James I. Following his death it was inherited by his daughter Isabel, and was renamed Holland House after she married Sir Henry Rich, 1st Earl of Holland in 1616 (he was executed in 1649 by Cromwell's puritans for his royalist activities). In the 19th century, Holland House became a hub of political and literary activity, visited by Disraeli and Lord Byron among others. It was severely damaged by bombs in 1940 and only the restored East Wing remains.

Walk 9

Globe

made by Nicholas Stone in 1629, they were built for the entrance gates to Holland House, but now form a grand entrance to Holland Park Opera. The piers are Doric columns on pedestals, above which are carved griffins holding the Rich and Cope Arms, which symbolise the union of the two families – see box, Holland House – Holland Park Opera (www.operahollandpark. com) performs a summer

season of open-air performances here under a temporary canopy, with the remains of the house as a backdrop.

Just past the piers are the remains of **Holland House** ㉓ (see box, page 111). It's possible to stay in this lovely old Jacobean building for less than the price of a cheap chain hotel, as there's now a youth hostel gloriously located in the East Wing, surrounding a private courtyard garden (for information see www.safestay.com/london-kensington-holland-park). From here go straight ahead and exit the park via the Duchess of Bedford's Walk entrance. At the end (by the junction with Campden Hill Road) are private Academy Gardens on the left, where there's an unusual sculpture of a slate **Globe** ㉔ by Joe Smith. The work measures 6ft (1.83m) in diameter and weighs around seven tonnes.

Turn left to walk up Campden Hill Road and turn right at the end to Notting Hill Gate, where there are some interesting sculptures amidst the urban sprawl. Walk east past the tube station entrance to see Nadim Karam's 2003 street sculpture **Carnival Elephant** ㉕ in front of Newcombe House (number 45). To the left, above Waterstone's bookshop (next door), are two more figures by Karam, a wild cat and a travelling carnival goer. On the wall to the right of the elephant is **The Climber** ㉖ by Peter Logan, which you could be forgiven for

Holland Park to High St Kensington

mistaking for an over-sized TV aerial. It's a wind sculpture made from climbing equipment, including ropes, pitons and alpenstock, and apparently 'represents the viewer's hopes and dreams as they climb through life's difficulties' (obviously!). Around 100m east along Notting Hill Gate, on the corner with Palace Gardens, is Václav Vokolek's stainless steel sculpture, **Haiku** 27 outside the Czech Embassy. It's composed of three pieces of stainless steel set against the harshness of the concrete wall behind, with seemingly random words cut into the metal, which are in fact a haiku (a Japanese verse form).

Retrace your steps past the Notting Hill Arts Club and go left down **Kensington Church Street** 28 (see box opposite). This is one of London's more interesting shopping streets, particularly for art and antiques enthusiasts; it even has its own website (www.antiques-london.com). A short way down turn left along Kensington Mall and continue to Palace Gardens Terrace, where you'll find the **Mall Tavern** 29 on your right – a good place for lunch. Retrace your steps, turn left onto

Food & Drink

13 **Holland Park Café:** A calm oasis providing a range of home-made seasonal food, including take-away snacks and lunch boxes for kids (8.30am-5.30pm, £).

29 **The Mall Tavern:** A Victorian gastropub off Kensington Church Street serving seasonal pub grub and Sunday roasts (noon-midnight, Sun noon-10.30pm, £-££).

34 **The Ivy Kensington Brasserie:** Offering an eclectic mix of modern British comfort food and international dishes, the Ivy on High Street Kensington provides casual dining, ranging from breakfast to dinner (020-3301 0500, Mon-Sat 8am-11/11.30pm, Sun 9am-10.30pm, £-££).

Carnival Elephant

Kensington Church Street and around half way down on the right, on the corner of Campden Street, is the Churchill Arms, a Fuller's pub that's a visual treat both inside and out (and a serial winner of the 'London in Bloom' competition).

At the end of Church Street turn left on Kensington High Street and walk east towards Kensington

St Mary Abbots

A splendid Victorian neo-Gothic church in Early English Style, St Mary Abbots occupies a site where a church has stood for some 1,000 years. In around 1100, Godfrey de Vere, the son of Aubrey de Vere who owned the manor of Kensington, was taken ill and cured (albeit briefly) by the abbot of the great Benedictine Abbey of St Mary at Abingdon. In gratitude the de Veres bequeathed the church in Kensington to the abbey, which was dedicated to St Mary in 1262 (rebuilt 1370). Two later churches proved too small for the congregation, and the current church was built in 1872 by the celebrated architect Sir George Gilbert Scott. It contains some notable treasures, including a 17th-century pulpit donated by William III and a monument carved by Grinling Gibbons for Sir Hans Sloane.

Palace Gardens, around 200m up on the left. This is one of the UK's most exclusive addresses, where some of the vast mansions are said to be worth over £100 million. The super-rich residents include the Russian and Israeli embassies so it isn't surprising that there are armed police checkpoints at both ends of the street. Just past Kensington Palace Gardens is Palace Avenue (before Kensington Gardens), the main entrance road for Kensington Palace. Note the Coade stone **Gate Piers** ㉚ , depicting a lion and a unicorn holding the Hanoverian coat of arms, believed to date from the early 19th century.

Return to Kensington Church Street, where on the western corner is the splendid **Kensington War Memorial** ㉛ outside **St Mary Abbots** ㉜ church (see box). Dating from 1922, it was designed by Major Hubert C. Corlette and sculpted by Frederick William Pomeroy. The main pillar is made of Portland stone with four finials with a winged angel between each on the upper part, topped by an ornately carved cross; however, the most striking feature is the lovely heavily-draped female figure (by Pomeroy) on the south face of the shaft.

Turn right after the church to Kensington Church Court, where St Mary Abbots School is on the right. Designed by Nicholas Hawksmoor (when he was Clerk of Works at Kensington Palace) and built in 1711-12, it was originally the Kensington Charity School. Nowadays the only reminder is Thomas Eustace's pair of fine stone **Charity Children** ㉝ statues on the façade. Just past the school is St Mary Abbot Gardens, a peaceful sanctuary just a few steps from the hustle and bustle of the High Street. Turn south along Kensington Church Walk back to the High

Charity Children

Holland Park to High St Kensington

Street, where on the left is the **Ivy Kensington Brasserie** 34 with its tempting all-day menu. Continue right along the High Street past the handsome Melli Bank building (1852), formerly the Central Library, and take the second right to Campden Hill Road.

Just up on the right is the 'new' **Kensington Central Library** ㉟ which opened in 1960. Built in imposing Neo-Renaissance style, it was unpopular to begin with but is now Grade II* listed. On the west side of the building in Phillimore Walk are statues on pedestals by William McMillan, including a lion on the left and a unicorn on the right, holding coats of arms. Two other McMillan pieces – high relief busts of Caxton and Chaucer within a wreath of leaves on a circular stone panel – are situated above the main entrances on the north side. McMillan also sculpted **Genius** ㊱, the bronze gilded hermaphrodite figure located on the roof, which is a cleverly disguised lightning conductor.

The library is your last stop. From here, return to Kensington High Street, turn left and cross over to the tube station – the end of the walk – which is surrounded by a tempting cornucopia of shops and restaurants.

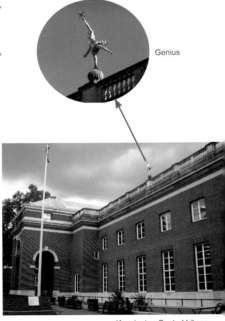

Genius

Kensington Central Library

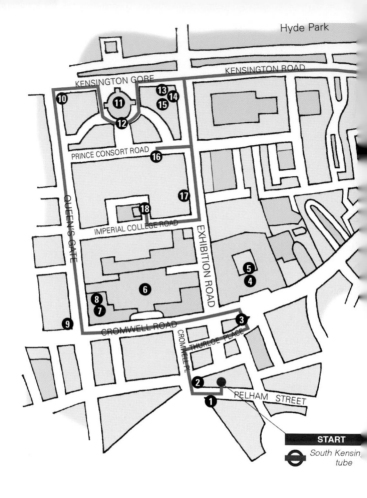

1. Béla Bartók Memorial
2. Muriel's Kitchen
3. Twelve Responses to Tragedy
4. Victoria & Albert Museum
5. V&A Café
6. Natural History Museum
7. Wildlfe Garden
8. Indian Ocean Tsunami Memorial
9. Lord Baden-Powell

10. Lord Robert Napier
11. Royal Albert Hall
12. Memorial to the Great Exhibition
13. Sir Clements Robert Markham
14. Dr David Livingstone
15. Sir Ernest Shackleton
16. Royal School of Mines
17. Queen Victoria
18. Queen's Tower

● Places of Interest ● Food & Drink

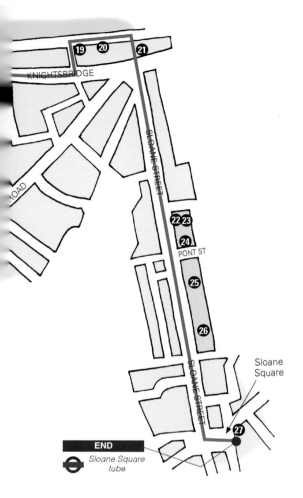

19 Pan or The Rush of Green
20 Search for Enlightenment
21 Triga
22 Volare
23 The Dancers

24 Cabmen's Shelter
25 Dancer with Bird
26 Girl with Doves
27 Colbert

South Kensington to Sloane Square

Distance: 3¾ miles (6 km)
Terrain: easy
Duration: 2-3 hours
Start: South Kensington tube
End: Sloane Square tube
Postcode: SW7 2NB

This walk commences in South Kensington in the Royal Borough of Kensington & Chelsea, an area that was largely undeveloped until the mid-19th century. Back then it supplied London with fruit and vegetables, whereas now it's home to some of the most desirable real estate in the world. It's popular with expatriates, particularly the French – the Lycée Français and Institut Français are both located here. 'South Ken' encompasses part of Cromwell Road – said to be named after Richard Cromwell, the son of Oliver Cromwell and his (brief) successor as Lord Protector – and Exhibition Road. This area was nicknamed Albertopolis, after Prince Albert, consort of Queen Victoria. It was Albert who was the driving force behind the decision to create a home for institutions dedicated to the arts and sciences, paving the way for the foundation of the museums, colleges and university you see today.

We visit three of Albert's enduring legacies, the Victoria & Albert Museum, Natural History Museum and Royal Albert Hall – all adorned with a wealth of sculptures – before heading east to Knightsbridge, one of London's most exclusive residential and retail enclaves, home to the world-famous department stores Harrods and Harvey Nichols. The last leg takes us south along Sloane Street in Belgravia – an area developed by the Cadogan family in the 18th and 19th centuries – before finishing in Sloane Square.

Royal Albert Hall

South Kensington to Sloane Square

Start Walking...

On leaving South Kensington tube station on Old Brompton Road, turn left and just across Pelham Street is the **Béla Bartók Memorial** ❶, commemorating the Hungarian composer (1881-1945). The 2004 statue, by Hungarian sculptor Imre Varga, is located some 100m northwest of 7 Sydney Place where the composer stayed (with Sir Duncan and Lady Wilson) on his visits to London. Cross back over Pelham Street and turn right up Cromwell Place, then bear right to Thurloe Place. If you fancy breakfast, lunch or a cuppa, pop into **Muriel's Kitchen** 2 just past the tube station on Cromwell Place.

Twelve Responses to Tragedy

Around 150m along Thurloe Place – on the left opposite Thurloe Square Garden – is the Yalta Memorial Garden which commemorates those people displaced by the Soviet and Yugoslav authorities as a result of the Yalta Conference, which took place in Crimea at the conclusion of the Second World War. At the heart of the garden is Angela Conner's poignant statue, **Twelve Responses to**

Victoria & Albert Museum

The Victoria and Albert Museum (usually abbreviated to the V&A) is the world's leading museum of art and design. Established in 1852 after the Great Exhibition of 1851, it was championed by Prince Albert who wanted a museum of applied arts that would inspire and educate people. Its immense and eclectic investment in decorative art takes in glass and ceramics, textiles and costumes, metalwork and jewellery, domestic items and furniture – and it's also rich in fine art. The permanent collection numbers over 2.2 million objects, of which only some 60,000 are displayed at any one time in 145 galleries. (For more information, see www.vam.ac.uk.)

Tragedy ❸ – which replaced an earlier statue (also by Conner) damaged by vandalism – consisting of a bronze bust of 12 conjoined heads of men, women and children mounted on a stone column on a brick plinth. From the garden, cross Cromwell Gardens to visit the **Victoria & Albert Museum** ❹ (free, see box), which officially opened in 1857 and is one of Britain's greatest national museums. Even if you don't have time to visit the museum, it's worth stopping for a drink or snack at the **V&A Café** 5 with its trio of glorious rooms, designed by three eminent Victorians – James Gamble, Edward J. Poynter and William Morris – and opened in 1868.

Walk 10

V&A Café

The museum's exterior is another treat, in particular the 'new' façade – built between 1899 and 1909 and designed by Sir Aston Webb. The design includes a wealth of sculptural ornaments to its exterior, including a statue of Queen Victoria supported by St George and St Michael over the great arch, with her Prince Consort Albert below, flanked by Edward VII and Queen Alexandra. The great archway itself is enriched with symbolic sculpture.

Distinguished sculptor Alfred Drury was chosen to lead the programme of decoration, along with other leading artists of the day, including George Frampton, William Silver Frith and Édouard Lantéri (along with some of his students). Together, they were commissioned to fashion Webb's patriotic vision of a pantheon of British artists in stone, each 7ft 9in (2.4m) tall. As a result, running along the entire length of the façade (and continuing along Exhibition Road) are 36 statues within niches, representing British painters, craftsmen, sculptors and architects. These included luminaries of the highest order – Millais, Constable, Hogarth,

Turner, Morris, Chippendale, Wedgwood, Wren and Inigo Jones – along with other craftsmen who, although lesser known today, were renowned in the 18th-19th centuries for their work in bookbinding, silversmithing and wood carving. Each statue is inscribed with the subject's name beneath his feet (no women are depicted!) and the sculptor's name to the right of the statue.

Continuing west along Cromwell Road, you come to another of the capital's classic collections, the **Natural History Museum** **6** (see box). This, too, has a richly-

South Kensington to Sloane Square

decorated façade including many animal carvings and gargoyles, although unlike most gargoyles – which tend to be grotesques with predominantly human or mythological form – these are intricately carved animals and, in some cases, prehistoric beasts. In the Darwin Centre garden, north of the **Wildlife Garden 7**, is the **Indian Ocean Tsunami Memorial 8** to victims of the 2004 tsunami, which killed an estimated 230,000-280,000 people. The memorial consists of a 115-tonne (French) granite monolith with a diagonal slice undercutting one corner, revealing a polished triangular face with an embossed dedication: In memory of all those who died in the Indian Ocean tsunami 26 December 2004.

Just past the museum, on the opposite side of Queen's Gate, is Don Potter's 1960 granite statue of **Lord Baden-Powell 9** (1857-1941), standing proudly outside Baden-Powell House. A British army general, Baden-Powell founded the Boy Scouts Association in 1908 and the Girl Guides in 1910. Turn right and

---

Royal Albert Hall

Designed by civil engineers Francis Fowke and Henry Y. D. Scott, and opened by Queen Victoria in 1871, the Royal Albert Hall (Grade I listed) is one of the capital's most treasured historic buildings; an ornate Italianate concert hall with a distinctive glass and wrought-iron dome rising to 135ft (41m). It was commissioned 'for the advancement of the arts and sciences and works of industry of all nations in fulfilment of the intention of Albert Prince Consort' – although Albert sadly died ten years before its completion. The hall seats 5,272 and hosts some 400 events a year, including classical music, rock and pop concerts, ballet, opera, film screenings with live orchestra, sports, awards ceremonies, community events, charity performances and banquets. You can take a tour of the hall, including exclusive access to the Royal Retiring Room (see www.royalalberthall.com/tickets/tours-and-exhibitions/group-tours).

---

walk north along Queen's Gate to the end facing Kensington Gardens, where there's a magnificent bronze equestrian statue of **Lord Robert Napier 10** (1810-1890), aka Lord Napier of Magdala, by Sir Joseph Edgar Boehm (unveiled in 1891). Field Marshal Napier had a long and distinguished army career, taking part in many campaigns, including the first and second Anglo-Sikh wars, the North-West Frontier, the Indian Mutiny and the Chinese Opium Wars. It was in Abyssinia (modern-day Ethiopia) that he achieved his greatest fame, leading a gruelling expedition to free hostages of Emperor Tewodros II of Ethiopia, for which he was rewarded with the title, Baron Napier of Magdala, after the Battle of Magdala which took place in the Emperor's mountain stronghold.

Turn right on Kensington Road, where just past the Royal College of Art and facing Kensington Gardens is the magnificent **Royal Albert Hall** ⑪ (see box, page 121). It's encircled by a mosaic frieze 800 feet (244m) in length covering an area of 5,200ft² (483m²); it's formed of foot-long slabs of mosaic tesserae and depicts 'The Triumph of Arts and Sciences', from music and painting to engineering. Opposite the hall's south entrance is Joseph Durham's **Memorial to the Great Exhibition** ⑫ of 1851, depicting Prince Albert surrounded by bronze female figures. It was installed in 1863 in the South Kensington Royal Horticultural Society Gardens and relocated here in 1893.

Heading east, just past the Royal Albert Hall is the HQ of the Royal Geographical Society (RGS), founded in 1830 for the advancement of geographical sciences. In the courtyard to the right of the entrance to Lowther Lodge is a bust of **Sir Clements Robert Markham** ⑬ (1830-1916), an English naval officer, geographer, explorer and writer. He was secretary of the RGS between 1863 and 1888 and served as the Society's president

for a further 12 years. In a niche in front of the building's lecture hall on Kensington Gore (near the corner with Exhibition Road) is a statue of **Dr David Livingstone** ⑭ (1813-1873), whose search for the source of the Nile – and meeting with Sir Henry Morton Stanley on the shores of Lake Tanganyika – earned him mythical status in his lifetime, although he was as much a missionary as an explorer. Sculpted in 1953 by Thomas Bayliss Huxley-Jones, the statue depicts the doctor leaning on his cane, cradling his Bible in his other hand, his coat over his arm.

Around the corner in Exhibition Road is Charles Sargeant

Queen's Tower

Standing 287ft (87m) tall, clad in Portland stone and topped with a copper-covered dome, the Queen's Tower is all that remains of the Imperial Institute, built to mark Queen Victoria's Golden Jubilee in 1887. The Imperial Institute was established by Royal Charter to undertake research into the resources and raw materials of the Empire, and to provide a meeting place for overseas visitors. Designed by Thomas Edward Collcutt in Neo-Renaissance style, the building originally had three towers, of which the central Queen's Tower was the largest. The Institute wasn't a great success and when Imperial College was expanded in the '50s, it was demolished. However, a public campaign, inspired by the then Poet Laureate, John Betjeman, saved the Queen's Tower.

South Kensington to Sloane Square

Shackleton

Jagger's statue of another famous explorer, **Sir Ernest Shackleton** ⓯ (1874-1922), portrayed in full cold-weather gear. Shackleton's reputation is based on a very British heroic failure: during his 1914 polar expedition to cross Antarctica, his ship the *Endeavour* was crushed in pack ice. It was Shackleton's leadership in extracting his crew without losing a man that made him a cult figure.

From the RGS turn right down Exhibition Road and right again along Prince Consort Road to the **Royal School of Mines** ⓰ building on the left. The school was established in 1851 as the Government School of Mines and Science Applied to the Arts. The current building, now occupied by Imperial College London, was designed by Sir Aston Webb and built in 1909-1913. The entrance is flanked by two memorials by Paul Raphael Montford; on the right is British gold and diamond magnate Alfred Beit (1853-1906) and on the left his business partner, German-born Julius Werner (1850-1912), both major benefactors of the school. Returning to Exhibition Road, next door to the Royal School of Mines is Imperial College London, which has a fine marble statue of **Queen Victoria** ⓱ in the main entrance (installed in 2006). It was previously located outside the Imperial Institute and later inside the **Queen's Tower** ⓲ (see box opposite) – the only remaining part of the Imperial Institute – where the statue's crown mysteriously vanished. To see the Tower, turn right along Imperial College Road and walk down to Queen's Lawn.

Retrace your steps along Exhibition Road and turn right on Kensington Road, heading east towards Knightsbridge. After 500m or so (just past the Dulgari

Food & Drink

② **Muriel's Kitchen:** A lively bistro near South Kensington tube station, Muriel's serves fresh seasonal produce (8am-11pm, Sun 10pm, £).

⑤ **V&A Café:** Hot dishes, sandwiches and cakes served up in the original Morris, Gamble and Poynter Rooms, which comprised the first museum 'café' in the world. The ornate tiling is reportedly modelled on Prince Albert's dairy at Windsor (10am-5pm, £).

㉗ **Colbert:** Classic Parisian all-day café (8am-11/11.30pm, Sun 10.30pm, £-££),

Pan/Rush of Green

Hotel), turn left up narrow Park Close to South Carriage Drive. Turn right and just along on the right is **Pan** or **The Rush of Green** ⑲, a group of sculptures set outside the entrance to One Hyde Park – the Candy Bros monument to the obscenely rich. It was the last work completed by Jacob Epstein before his death in 1959 and depicts a long-limbed family – father, mother, son and dog – rushing towards Hyde Park, encouraged by the Greek god Pan playing his pipes. A little further along is **Search for Enlightenment** ⑳ by Simon Gudgeon, unveiled in 2012. The bronze sculpture depicts two human profiles, one male and one female, facing Hyde Park.

Search for Enlightenment

Continue along South Carriage Drive and go right on Serpentine Walk to Knightsbridge. Turn right and cross over to Brompton Road, then follow the Burberry store round to the right to Knightsbridge Green (which is not especially green). Here, above the entrance to One Knightsbridge Green (formerly Caltex House), is **Triga** ㉑ , an abstract trio of racehorses. Sculpted in 1957 by Czech Franta Belsky, it recalls the racehorses that were bought and sold on this site, which was occupied by Tattersalls bloodstock auctioneers for almost 75 years. Retrace your steps to Knightsbridge tube station and turn right into Sloane Street, one of London's most luxurious shopping streets and home to Harvey Nichols department store.

Cabmen's Shelters

Established throughout London in the 19th century, these shelters served teetotal refreshments to tired hansom cab drivers (as they still do today). They were intended as an alternative to pubs, where cabbies invariably took refuge in inclement weather (any excuse) with inevitable consequences!

Head south down Sloane Street and just after the Jumeirah Carlton Tower is Cadogan Place, about which Charles Dickens wrote: 'Cadogan Place is the one slight bond that joins two great extremes; it is the connecting link between the aristocratic

South Kensington to Sloane Square

pavements of Belgrave Square and the barbarism of Chelsea… The people in Cadogan Place look down upon Sloane Street and think Brompton low.' Cadogan Place was laid out by Henry Holland from 1777 and gives its name to Cadogan Place Gardens, a welcome swathe of green. Sadly, the gardens are private, although you can visit during Open Squares Weekend (www.opensquares.org) in June and under the National Garden Scheme (www.ngs.org. uk).

The Dancers

It's worth timing your visit for when the gardens are open as they're home to a number of sculptures. In the North Garden – originally created by Humphry Repton in 1806 – is **Volare 22**, a striking aluminium statue by Lorenzo Quinn dating from 2011. It also features one of three sculptures here by David Wynne created in 1971-74: **The Dancers 23** features an entwined man and woman dancing with abandon, standing on a raised octagonal granite plinth.

To the south of the North Garden in Pont Street is a

Victorian **Cabmen's Shelter 24** ((see box opposite), one of only around a dozen remaining. In the main central garden is Wynne's **Dancer with Bird 25**, created in 1974, depicting a girl standing on a square granite plinth, while in the South Garden is **Girl with Doves 26**, a female nude figure on a stepped granite plinth with her hands above her head and five doves fluttering between them. One of the strengths of Wynne's work is his depiction of movement, which is well illustrated in this piece, as it appears that the birds are flying unsupported.

Continue along Sloane Street to Sloane Square, and the end of the walk – Sloane Square tube station is in the southeast corner. If you're peckish or fancy a drink, just a few steps away is **Colbert 27**, with Art Nouveau, Art Deco and Victorian features – and excellent French bistro food.

Volare

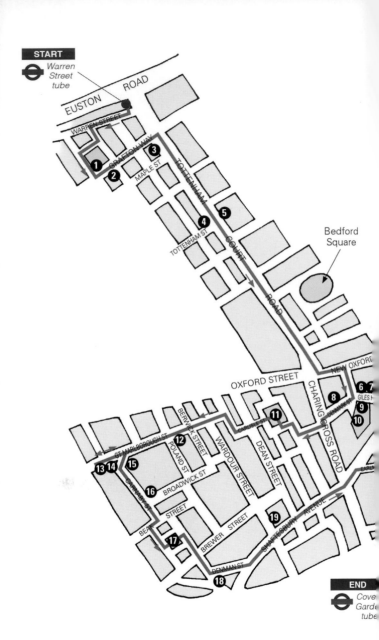

START
Warren
Street
tube

EUSTON ROAD

WARREN STREET

GRAFTON WAY

MAPLE ST

TOTTENHAM COURT ROAD

1
2
3
4
5

TOTTENHAM ST

Bedford
Square

NEW OXFORD

OXFORD STREET

CHARING CROSS ROAD

GILES H

DENMARK ST

6 **7**
8
9
10
11

BERWICK STREET

CARLISLE ST

WARDOUR STREET

DEAN STREET

GT MARLBOROUGH ST

POLAND ST

12

13 **14** **15**

CARNABY ST

BROADWICK STREET

16

EARL

SHAFTESBURY AVENUE

BEAK STREET

BREWER STREET

17

19

DENMAN ST

18

END
Cove
Garde
tube

WALK 11

Places of Interest   Food & Drink

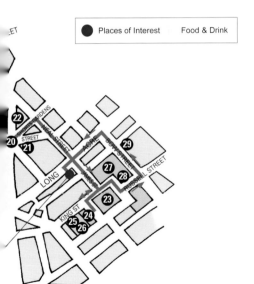

Fitzrovia to Covent Garden

Distance: 3½ miles (5½ km)
Terrain: easy
Duration: 2-3 hours
Start: Warren Street tube
End: Covent Garden tube
Postcode: NW1 3AA

FITZROVIA TO COVENT GARDEN

This walk takes in a succession of statues and sculptures, from monarchs' memorials to modern art, as well as some beautiful murals. We begin in the famously bohemian district of Fitzrovia – situated between Bloomsbury and Marylebone – an area that, until the end of the 19th century belonged to the Dukes of Grafton (family name FitzRoy). After a stroll down Tottenham Court Road, a hotspot for consumer electronics, white goods and furniture, we head to the district of St Giles – once one of London's most infamous rookeries (slums), now home to an upmarket piazza. Then it's along Denmark Street, beloved by musicians, to Soho Square with its celebrated statue of Charles II.

Carnaby Street

From the square we go west through Soho towards Regent Street, to explore the famous Liberty London store and check out Carnaby Street. Since the '60s this street has been a fashion mecca – from mods and hippies, skinheads and punks to the street style fashionistas of today – and remains central to the city's culture. Our sojourn in Soho also takes in Shaftesbury Avenue, named after the 7th Earl of Shaftesbury – the hub of London's theatre district – and the tranquillity of St Anne's Churchyard off Wardour Street.

We end the walk in Covent Garden, which was developed from the 16th century by the Russell family (the Earls, later Dukes, of Bedford) who held the land until 1918. The site of London's fruit and vegetable market until 1974, it's now a popular shopping and entertainment district, and home to the Royal Opera House.

Start Walking...

From Warren Street tube station bear right and head west along Warren Street and turn left on Fitzroy Street to Fitzroy Square Garden. The square is private but in the southwest corner there's a good view through the railings of Naomi Blake's **View** ❶ , which was unveiled to celebrate the Queen's Silver Jubilee in 1977. Blake specialises in sculptures of embryonic and human forms which are said to 'express her experience of the holocaust and dedication to understanding between faiths'. Walk east to the corner of Fitzroy Street to see (in an alcove) a statue of **Francisco de Miranda** ❷ (1750-1816), a modern replica of an 1895 sculpture by Rafael de la Cova. General Miranda was a Venezuelan military leader and revolutionary who had an English wife and lived from 1802 to 1810 at 58 Grafton Way (aka Casa Miranda), opposite the statue and marked by a blue plaque.

Walk along Grafton Way and turn right onto Tottenham Court Road. A short distance along on the right is **TAP Coffee** ❸ , a nice bright spot for a latte or flat white. Continue south and on the right, just before Goodge Street tube station, is Whitfield Gardens, home to the iconic **Fitzrovia Mural** ❹ (see box). Opposite the gardens is the flagship **Heal's** ❺ home store; completed in 1854, it's one of the West End's most architecturally important buildings, designed in Venetian Palazzo style by James Morant Lockyer. The building was extended in 1916, when a stunning spiral staircase by Cecil Brewer was added.

Fitzrovia Mural

Commissioned by Camden Council and created in 1980 by artists Simon Barber (who painted the bottom half) and Mick Jones (who did the top), the Fitzrovia Mural is regarded as one of London's most important outdoor artworks. It records the life of the local community, including portraits of local people. The mural has deteriorated over the years and was being restored in 2018 – with luck this will be completed by the time you see it.

Fitzrovia Mural

Continue along Tottenham Court Road to the junction with Oxford Street, where you go left and cross over to the south side of New Oxford Street. From here take the first right to Earnshaw Street just past the Centre Point tower

Walk 11

Ob 08

block – vacant for many years, it became known as London's 'empty skyscraper' – and the second left into Central Saint Giles Piazza, one of London's more colourful mixed-use developments. In the piazza is Steven Gontarski's (2008) striking bright red abstract sculpture **Ob 08 ❻** , standing over 16ft (5m), made of painted and lacquered glass-fibre-reinforced plastic. At the southern entrance is **William ❼** , a 10ft (3m) bronze by Rebecca Warren. A fluid, anonymous figure (i.e. shapeless blob), it's intended to 'speak of the ever-shifting present' rather than the past – the exact opposite of most public sculptures.

Exit onto St Giles High Street and go right to **Denmark Street ❽** (see box). On the left is **St Giles-in-the-Fields ❾** , aka the Poets' Church – the children of Lord Byron and Percy Bysshe Shelley

and Mary Shelley were baptised here. There has been a chapel on this site since 1101 when Queen Matilda, wife of Henry I, founded a leper hospital here (part of the former hospital's site is now the delightful Phoenix Garden). The present Palladian-style church was built in 1731-33 and contains a number of memorials. If you're peckish, just past the church on Denmark Street is a branch of the excellent café chain **Fernandez & Wells ❿** .

Continue to the end of Denmark Street and cross Charing Cross Road, then turn right along Manette Street to Greek Street and right again towards

Charles

Soho Square. Dating back to the 17th century, it was originally called King Square after **Charles II ⓫** ; a statue of the monarch by Danish sculptor Caius Gabriel Cibber (1630-1700) stands in the middle of the square. The statue was installed here in 1681, removed in 1875 for work on the square and wasn't replaced until 1938. Soho Square is also noted for its two-storey, half-timbered 'gardener's hut' – part tool-shed, part arbour – which is Grade II listed. On the south side there's a bench commemorating Kirsty MacColl (1959-2000), killed by

---

Denmark Street

Associated with British popular music since the '50s, first through its publishers and later its recording studios and music shops, Denmark Street was once the UK's 'Tin Pan Alley'. A blue plaque unveiled in 2014 commemorates the street's importance to popular music. It's now being redeveloped, but remains the best place in London for independent music shops, particularly for guitars.

powerboat while scuba diving
n Mexico, who wrote the song
Soho Square for her album *Titanic
Days*. Dedicated by her fans, the
bench is inscribed with the lyrics,
'One day I'll be waiting there / no
empty bench in Soho Square'.

Liberty London

Synonymous with luxury and
outstanding design since its launch in
1875, Liberty is one of London's most
iconic stores. The legacy of founder
Arthur Lasenby Liberty, it stands for
integrity, value, quality and, above
all, beautiful design – not least the
building itself. The timber-framed,
mock-Tudor store was built in 1924
and constructed almost entirely from
the timbers of two old warships, *HMS
Hindustan* and *HMS Impregnable*.

Leave the square via the
western exit onto Carlisle Street,
go right at the end to Great Chapel
Street and then left to Hollen
Street, which runs into Noel
Street. On the left, just before
Poland St, is another fine mural:
Ode to the West Wind 12, which
refers to a poem written in 1819
by Percy Bysshe Shelley. Shelley
lived for a while around the corner
from the mural at 15 Poland
Street. The mural was painted in
1989 by the London Wall Mural
group led by Louise Vines, and
depicts a large tree (that has split
in half) with a person sitting to one
side reading a book. Continue

along Noel Street into Great
Marlborough Street, keep walking
west and just past Carnaby Street
is **Liberty London** 13 (see box),
one of the city's most popular and
iconic stores. Note the golden
Weathervane 14 on top of the
building, a replica of the Pilgrim
Fathers' ship, the *Mayflower*.

Retrace your steps to Carnaby
Street, where, on the corner
of Great Marlborough Street
and Foubert's Place, is the
Shakespeare's Head 15, a
traditional Greene King pub.
It dates back to 1735 and
allegedly has connections to the
Bard, illustrated by a statue of
Shakespeare leaning out of a
window on the corner of the pub;
it has been there since 1910 and
lost a hand to a bomb during the
Second World War.

Ode to the West Wind

From here go under the arched
entrance to Carnaby Street, which
was the fashion hub of Swinging
London in the '60s. Around
three-quarters of the way down
on the left, just around the corner

Walk 11

in Broadwick Street, is another superb mural, **The Spirit of Soho** 16 (see box). Broadwick Street was the location of the infamous John Snow Water Pump, which led to a cholera outbreak in 1854 that killed over 600 people; the pump was named after the physician who stopped the outbreak simply by removing its handle, and hence access to the contaminated water.

At the end of Carnaby Street, go right on Beak Street and left on Upper John Street to Golden Square: in the centre is a statue of **George II** 17 which was created by John Nost ca. 1724 and erected here in 1753. From the square go south along Lower James Street and cross over to Sherwood Street, and as the road bears right you come to **Brasserie Zédel** 18 , an excellent choice for a tasty, good-value lunch. A few steps back up Sherwood Street turn right into Denman Street and left on Shaftesbury Avenue. Here, you pass a succession of famous theatres – the Lyric, Apollo, Gielgud and Queen's – all of which display various plaques.

Just past the Queen's Theatre turn left down Wardour Street to the hidden oasis of **St Anne's Churchyard Gardens** 19 , where there are a number of memorials. These include a First World War memorial (with further names added for WWII); a plaque to David Williams (1738-1816), founder of the Royal Literary Fund; a plaque to Theodore, the dethroned King of Corsica (1694-1756), and a granite drinking fountain commemorating local resident George Maule Allen (1855-1889). There are also plaques to writers Dorothy L. Sayers (1893-1957), who was a churchwarden (her ashes are buried beneath the tower) and William Hazlitt (1778-1830), a brilliant essayist now largely forgotten.

Spirit of Soho

Seven Dials

3 **TAP Coffee:** Excellent coffee in a pared-down, relaxing space (Mon-Fri 7.30am-7pm, Sat 10am-6pm, closed Sun, £).

10 **Fernandez & Wells:** Celebrated chain serving superb coffee, sandwiches and Camden Brewery's draught beers (Mon-Tue, 8am-9pm, Wed-Fri 11pm, Sat 10am-10pm, Sun 10am-5pm, £).

15 **Shakespeare's Head:** Handsome traditional Soho pub with a beer garden (daily 11am-10pm, Sun 9pm, £).

18 **Brasserie Zédel:** Grand Parisian brasserie, serving classic French cuisine at affordable prices (11.30am-midnight, Sun 11pm, £).

areas. Seven Dials is a road junction where no fewer than seven streets converge, at the centre of which is a circular island containing a pillar bearing six sundials, commissioned before a late addition to the original planned six roads. On the east side of Seven Dials and Earlham Street is the **Cambridge Theatre** **21**, which has a lovely interior bronze frieze (1930) by Antony Gibbons Grinling, depicting nude figures on the themes of dance, music and drama; the topic continues into the main foyer, with more dancing nudes, marble pilaster uplighters and concealed lighting. From Seven Dials take Shorts Gardens and turn left

From the gardens return to Shaftesbury Avenue and continue eastwards to the junction with Charing Cross Road, where the Palace Theatre is on the left. Cross over the junction and take Earlham Street on the right, which leads to **Seven Dials** **20** in Covent Garden, one of London's most historic and atmospheric

Neal's Yard

Living Sculpture

> ### Neal's Yard
>
> Named after its 17th-century developer, Thomas Neale (who also created Seven Dials), Neal's Yard is one of London's most colourful 'streets', quite literally, as some of the buildings are painted in startling bright colours. Today's yard was created in the late '70s when the area was derelict and rents were low (Covent Garden Market had just upped sticks to south London) and an entrepreneur called Nicholas Saunders rented a warehouse here. With the emphasis upon alternative, healthy living, Saunders opened a wholefood shop, which was followed by a dairy, a café and an apothecary specialising in alternative remedies. Neal's Yard is now an international name.

through its long connection with the theatre and even has its own in-house theatre company.

Painter JMW Turner and William S Gilbert (of Gilbert & Sullivan fame) are among the many prominent people baptised at St Paul's, while among those buried here are novelist Samuel Butler, Thomas Arne (composer of *Rule Britannia*) and the woodcarver Grinling Gibbons, while memorials are dedicated to Charlie Chaplin, Boris Karloff and Vivien Leigh, among others. In the churchyard are

into **Neal's Yard** 22 (see box), a delightful backwater secreted between Shorts Gardens and Monmouth Street.

From Neal's Yard retrace your steps to Shorts Gardens and go left and then right on Neal Street to Long Acre. Cross over Long Acre and head down James Street, past Floral Street, and go right at the end to King Street where, just past the Apple store on the right-hand corner, is the

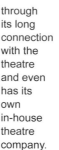

colonnaded Piazza building of **Covent Garden Market** 23 . Just west of the market is the beautiful church of **St Paul's Covent Garden** 24 , designed by Inigo Jones and consecrated in 1638; it's known as the Actors Church

Conversion of St Paul

Bruce Denny's 2010 equestrian statue of the **Conversion of St Paul** 25 , Philip Thomason's 1995 **Neptune Fountain** 26 and a Diamond Jubilee Memorial (aka 'Covent Garden maze') consisting of a small brick labyrinth encircling a relief of an over-sized coin.

Covent Garden Market is one of the city's most popular attractions

Fitzrovia to Covent Garden

Royal Opera House

This is the third theatre built on this site, the previous two having been destroyed by fire in 1808 and 1856. The first theatre – the Theatre Royal – was constructed in 1732 and the first ballet performed in 1734. The current building was designed by Edward Middleton Barry and dates from 1858, although only the façade, foyer, and auditorium (Grade I listed) are original; almost every other element dates from an extensive reconstruction in the 1990s. The theatre became the Royal Opera House in 1892 and today is home to the Royal Opera, the Royal Ballet and the Orchestra of the Royal Opera House.

and is actually a number of different markets, which vary according to the day of the week (see www.coventgardenlondonuk. com/markets). On weekends the Piazza is a good place to see one of London's best free spectacles: living statues. For the uninitiated, a living statue is a silent and perfectly still person, often dressed and painted head to toe in gold or silver. It's hard to imagine how they maintain their poses for hours on end (apparently meditation, Pilates and yoga all help), often in gravity-defying positions without any visible means of support.

From the Apple store follow the colonnade around the edge of the market to Russell Street and walk up to Bow Street to visit the **Royal Opera House** ㉗ (see box). On the side of the Opera House

overlooking Russell Street is Yinka Shonibare's 2012 **Globe Head Ballerina** ㉘ , featuring a life-sized, fibre-glass spinning ballerina encased within a giant 'snow globe'; the ballerina is based on a famous photograph of Margot Fonteyn. On a similar theme, just past the Opera House on Bow Street, at the entrance to Broad Court on the right, is Enzo Plazzotta's lovely bronze **Young Dancer** ㉙ , unveiled in 1988. Italian-born Plazzotta spent his working life in London and is best remembered for his fascination with and study of movement in bronze – the human form, horses, ballerinas and female studies – many of which adorn London's streets. Continue along Bow Street and turn left into Long Acre, where Covent Garden tube station – and the end of the walk – is a short way along on your left.

Young Dancer & Royal Opera House

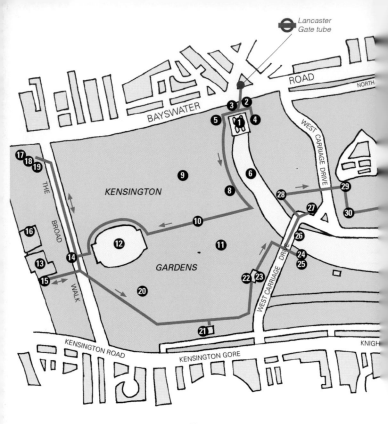

Lancaster Gate tube

ROAD

NORTH

WEST CARRIAGE DRIVE

BAYSWATER

KENSINGTON

GARDENS

THE BROAD WALK

KENSINGTON ROAD

KENSINGTON GORE

WEST CARRIAGE DRIVE

KNIGH

1. Italian Gardens
2. Italian Gardens Café
3. Queen Anne's Alcove
4. Jenner
5. Two Bears Fountain
6. Long Water
7. Serpentine
8. Peter Pan
9. Speke's Monument
10. Physical Energy
11. Queen Caroline's Temple
12. Round Pond
13. Kensington Palace
14. Queen Victoria
15. William III

16. The Orangery
17. Diana, Princess of Wales Memorial Playground
18. Elfin Oak
19. Time Flies
20. Bandstand
21. Albert Memorial
22. Serpentine Gallery
23. Diana, Princess of Wales
24. Isis Sculpture
25. Diana, Princess of Wales Memorial Fountain
26. Serpentine Bridge
27. Serpentine Sackler Gallery
28. Henry Moore Arch
29. Hudson Memorial Bird Sanctuary
30. Marble Arch

● Places of Interest   ○ Food & Drink

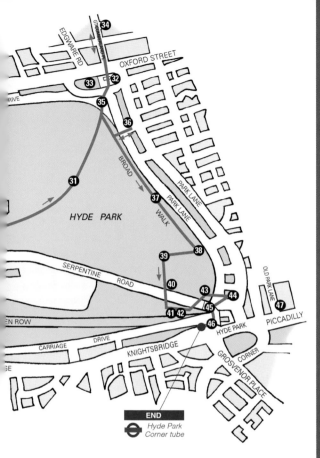

31 Norwegian War Memorial
32 Reformers' Tree
33 Still Water
34 Raoul Wallenberg
35 Speakers' Corner
36 Animals in War Memorial
37 Joy of Life Fountain
38 7th July Memorial
39 Little Nell

40 Cavalry Memorial
41 Huntress
42 Boy and Dolphin
43 Achilles
44 Lord Byron
45 Queen Elizabeth Gate
46 Hyde Park Screen
47 Rose & Crown

Hyde Park & Kensington Gardens

Distance: 6½ miles (10½ km)
Terrain: easy
Duration: 3-4 hours
Start: Lancaster Gate tube
End: Hyde Park Corner tube
Postcode: W2 4QH

HYDE PARK & KENSINGTON GARDENS

Historic Hyde Park and Kensington Gardens are two of the city's eight ancient royal parks, home to a wealth of famous monuments and memorials, many associated with the monarchy. Hyde Park is the second-largest of central London's royal parks – extending to 350 acres (142ha) – and was created in 1536 when Henry VIII seized land belonging to Westminster Abbey to create a deer park. It opened to the public in 1637 and since the 19th century has been a popular venue for free speech and demonstrations – Speakers' Corner in the northeast of the park was officially established as a place of opinion and debate in 1872. The park is also a venue for large-scale festivals and rock concerts.

Kensington Gardens were formerly the grounds of Nottingham House, which became Kensington Palace when William III acquired it in 1689. Originally part of Hyde Park, the gardens have been a separate green space since the 1730s and cover 275 acres (111ha). They were first opened to the public in 1733 and are home to London's most magnificent public work of art, the Albert Memorial, unveiled in 1872.

Hyde Park

Hyde Park & Kensington Gardens

Start Walking…

From Lancaster Gate tube station, cross Bayswater Road and enter Kensington Gardens via the Marlborough Gate, from where you have a glorious view of the **Italian Gardens** ❶ (see box) at the top of the Long Water. To the left of the entrance, **The Italian Gardens' Café** 2 is a handy spot to grab a drink or snack before starting the walk. Just past the café is **Queen Anne's Alcove** ❸ , designed by Sir Christopher Wren in 1705 for the queen's formal south garden, just south of Kensington Palace, but moved here in 1867. The shelter opposite the café is the gardens' former pump house; designed by Sir Charles Barry, it contained the steam engine that powered the fountains. Look for Victoria and Albert's initials on the walls and the beautiful decoration of relief carvings and imaginary figures.

Italian Gardens

The ornamental water gardens – created in 1860 to a design by James Pennethorne at the instigation of Prince Albert – are based on similar gardens at Osborne House on the Isle of Wight (one of Victoria's favourite homes). The gardens are an over-the-top confection with four main basins, featuring central rosettes carved in Carrara marble, a Portland stone and white marble Tazza Fountain, and a collection of stone statues and urns by John Thomas in five main designs: a swan's breast, woman's head, ram's head, dolphin and an oval.

Jenner

Follow the path around the eastern side of the gardens, where you see William Calder Marshall's 1858 bronze of **Jenner** ❹ ; Dr Edward Jenner (1749-1823) was the pioneer of the smallpox vaccine and is often called 'the father of immunology'.

Return to the top of the gardens and go west, where just past the Marlborough Gate entrance is David Wood's adorable **Two Bears Fountain** ❺ , featuring a bronze statue of two bears embracing. It was installed in 1939 to mark 80 years of the Metropolitan Drinking Fountain and Cattle Trough Association; however, the original proved irresistible to thieves and was replaced with this recast copy in 1970. From the fountain, follow the path south along the western edge of the **Long Water** ❻ that forms the northern 'tail' of the **Serpentine** ❼ , the lake that partly divides Hyde Park from Kensington Gardens. The Serpentine is an artificial lake and was created in 1730 for Queen

Peter Pan Statue

Erected in 1912, the statue by Sir George Frampton was commissioned and paid for by J.M. Barrie, creator of Peter Pan, the 'boy who wouldn't grow up'. Peter Pan is depicted playing his pipe, surrounded by fairies and woodland creatures. Barrie chose the location himself, claiming it's the spot where Peter landed in *Peter Pan in Kensington Gardens*. Today, it's one of London's most popular statues, beloved by generations of children.

Caroline (wife of George II) from a string of natural ponds along the River Westbourne. Around a third of the way down the Long Water you come to a celebrated bronze statue of **Peter Pan** ❽ (see box) overlooking the lake.

From here, go west to Philip Hardwick's **Speke Monument** ❾ , located near the junction of Lancaster and Budge's Walks. Made of red granite, it's dedicated to John Hanning Speke (1827-1864), the explorer who discovered Lake Victoria and led expeditions to find the source of the Nile. From here head south down Lancaster Walk to George Frederic Watts' impressive sculpture, **Physical Energy** ❿ , a large bronze depicting a naked man astride a horse, shielding his eyes from the sun. To the southeast is **Queen Caroline's Temple** ⓫ – dating from 1734-5 and attributed to William Kent – a

neo-classical style summerhouse overlooking the Long Water east of Lancaster Walk.

From Physical Energy head west to the **Round Pond** ⓬ , a 7-acre (2.8ha) ornamental lake created in 1730 by George II, popular with model yacht enthusiasts (and waterfowl). To the west of the pond, just past the Broad Walk, is **Kensington Palace** ⓭ (see box opposite). One of London's best-preserved palaces, it's where Queen Victoria was born and lived until her accession to the throne in 1837 at the age of 18. In front of the palace opposite the Round Pond is a marble statue of **Queen Victoria** ⓮ (1819-1901), designed by her daughter Princess Louise (Duchess of Argyll) in 1893, depicting Victoria in her coronation robes in 1837 aged just 18.

Just beyond the south gate of the palace on Dial Walk is Heinrich Baucke's bronze of **William III** ⓯ (1650-1702), presented to Edward VII by his nephew, the German Kaiser Wilhelm II in 1907. William chose to live at Kensington Palace because the air was cleaner

Physical Energy

Hyde Park & Kensington Gardens

Kensington Palace Gardens

conservation that's expected to take up to three years.

A little further on, in the northwest corner of the gardens, is the **Diana, Princess of Wales Memorial Playground** ⓘ, opened in 2000. Nearby, opposite the Broadwalk

...han at Whitehall and better for ...is asthma. Return to the Broad ...Valk and turn left, and just past ...he palace is **The Orangery** ⓰, ...nce the setting for Queen Anne's ...ophisticated court entertainment, ...vith soaring ceilings and classical ...8th-century architecture. It's now ... popular restaurant, although ...t closed in 2018 for renovation/

Queen Victoria & Kensington Palace

Café, is Ivor Innes' **Elfin Oak** ⓲, a much-loved sculpture dating from 1930 made from the hollow trunk of an ancient oak tree, carved with fairies, elves and animals. In the southeast of the playground is **Time Flies** ⓳, a clock tower and drinking fountain topped with a weathervane depicting a bird with outstretched wings.

Retrace your steps along the Broad Walk past the Round Pond, where you take the diagonal path that runs south of the **Bandstand** ⓴, installed in 1931 and designed by J. Markham of the Office of Works. The path brings you out on Flower Walk, where around 150m along on the right is the magnificent **Albert Memorial** ㉑ (see box, page 142), a tremendous artistic tour de force and London's grandest monument. From the memorial

Kensington Palace

Kensington Palace has been a residence of British royals since 1689 and has a fascinating historical and archaeological heritage. It was built in the early 17th century for the Earl of Nottingham and was purchased in 1689 by William III and his wife Mary II. For many people it's inextricably linked with the late Diana, Princess of Wales, and the vast sea of floral tributes spreading out from the gates following her death in 1997. Both of her sons and their families – William and Catherine, the Duke and Duchess of Cambridge, and Harry and Meghan, the Duke and Duchess of Sussex – live there now. You can access the spectacular palace gardens, which include the Princess Diana Memorial Garden, from Kensington Gardens free of charge, although there's a fee to visit the palace. (See www.hrp.org.uk/kensington-palace for information.)

Albert Memorial

Situated in the south of Kensington Gardens – opposite the Royal Albert Hall – the Albert memorial commemorates Queen Victoria's adored husband, Albert, Prince Consort (1819-1861), who died of typhoid fever aged just 42. Unveiled in 1872, the grand, high-Victorian Gothic extravaganza was designed by Sir Gilbert Scott and influenced by the series of 13th-century Eleanor Crosses (Charing Cross being the most well known) and other statues in Edinburgh and Manchester. It incorporates a gilt-bronze figure of Albert by John Henry Foley and celebrates the achievements of the Victorian age and empire (and Albert's passions and interests), with massive marble sculptures of the continents and a delicately carved frieze of 'artists'.

The seated Albert is depicted holding the catalogue of the Great Exhibition, staged in Hyde Park in 1851, which he inspired and helped to organise. Marble figures representing Europe, America, Asia and Africa stand at each corner, while higher up are allegorical sculptures representing agriculture, commerce, engineering and manufactures. Still further up, near the top, are gilded bronze statues of the angels and virtues. The mosaics on each side (beneath the canopy) were designed by Clayton and Bell and manufactured in Murano, Venice.

Around the base of the memorial encircling the podium is the 210ft (64m) Frieze of Parnassus – named after Mount Parnassus, the favourite resting place of the muses in ancient Greek mythology – which contains 169 life-size, full-length sculptures reflecting Albert's enthusiasm for the arts. Henry Hugh Armstead carved the 80 figures of painters, musicians and poets on the memorial's south and east sides, while John Birnie Philip carved the 89 figures of sculptors and architects (plus two generic figures) on the west and north sides. You can take a tour of the memorial to see the frieze and other fine details up close (tel. 020-8969 0104 to book).

Mosaic

Prince Albert

Albert Memorial

Americas Group

Asia Group

ontinue along the East Albert Lawn path to Mount Gate and ake the path to the **Serpentine Gallery** ㉒ . Housed in a classical 1934 tea pavilion, the gallery is one of London's most important showcases for contemporary art. In summer the gallery's lawn is the venue for the Serpentine Gallery Pavilion commission, an annual programme of temporary structures by internationally acclaimed architects and designers (see www.serpentinegalleries.org for information). Ian Hamilton Finlay's **Memorial to Diana, Princess of Wales** ㉓ is located in the gallery's forecourt – Diana (1961-1997) was a patron of the gallery – in the form of a plaque set into the ground inscribed with the names of the trees found in Kensington Gardens.

From the gallery, cross over West Carriage Drive – which forms part of the border between Kensington Gardens and Hyde Park – and follow the path along the Serpentine's edge to see Simon Gudgeon's **Isis Sculpture** ㉔ , aka Serenity, a striking bronze inspired by the Egyptian goddess of nature. Opposite the sculpture is the **Diana, Princess of Wales Memorial Fountain** ㉕ , designed by Kathryn Gustafson and opened in 2004. The fountain aims to reflect Diana's life, flowing from the highest point in two directions as it cascades, swirls and bubbles before meeting in a calm pool at the bottom. Return to West Carriage Drive and cross over **Serpentine Bridge** ㉖ to

Serpentine Sackler Gallery

A sister gallery of the Serpentine Gallery (both offer free entrance), the striking Sackler Gallery was designed by prize-winning architect Zaha Hadid and opened in 2013. It's housed in a former 1805 gunpowder store and presents world-renowned exhibitions of art, architecture and design throughout the year. The Sackler is home to the Chucs Serpentine restaurant with an all-day menu.

the **Serpentine Sackler Gallery** ㉗ (see box).

Leave the gallery and turn right towards the eastern edge of the Long Water, where after around 100m you come to the **Henry Moore Arch** ㉘ sited alongside the lake. This 20ft (6m) high travertine marble sculpture, weighing 37 tonnes, was donated by Moore in 1980, and perfectly frames a view of Kensington Palace. Due east from the arch is the **Hudson Memorial Bird Sanctuary** ㉙ , a carved stone memorial by Sir Jacob Epstein (with engravings by Eric Gill) commemorating the 19th-century writer and naturalist William Henry Hudson (1841-1922), who helped establish the Royal Society for the Protection of Birds. Installed in 1924, the

Isis

Walk 12

carving represents Rima, the child goddess of nature who featured in Hudson's 1904 novel *Green Mansions*.

From here cut south across Hyde Park to see the **Norwegian War Memorial** ㉚ – in an area known as the Cockpit, just north of the Serpentine – consisting of a large pre-Cambrian granite boulder mounted on three smaller stones. It was presented to Britain by the Royal Norwegian Navy and Norwegian Merchant Fleet in 1978 as a thank you for British support during the Second World War. From the memorial follow the diagonal path northeast past the Rangers Lodge and the Lookout to a major crossroads where, in the centre, is a circular black and white mosaic from

Still Water

2000. It marks the spot where the **Reformers' Tree** ㉛ once stood, a noble oak that was the focus of protests in 1866 by the Reform League which campaigned for all adult men to be given the right to vote.

From the mosaic take the diagonal path northeast to **Marble Arch** ㉜ (see box), a white Carrara marble monument designed by John Nash, that once housed one of London's smallest police stations. A circular plaque nearby claims to mark the exact spot of the Tyburn Tree gallows – with the words 'The Site of Tyburn Tree' – a place of public execution from 1196 to 1783 (it's estimated that between 40,000 and 60,000 people died here). A short distance away, to the northwest of Marble Arch (at 8 Hyde Park Place), the Tyburn Convent is dedicated to the memory of martyrs executed here (and elsewhere) for their Catholic faith. In the west of the Marble Arch traffic island is a changing display of statues and also the permanent home of Nic Fiddian-Green's **Still Water** ㉝, a giant bronze horse's head (33ft/10m, weighing 6 tonnes) installed in 2011.

Before returning to the park, it's worth making a short detour up Great Cumberland Place to Wallenberg Place on the right, to see Philip Jackson's magnificent statue of Swede **Raoul Wallenberg** ㉞ (b. 1912,

Hyde Park & Kensington Gardens

eath unrecorded). Wallenberg helped save tens of thousands of Jews from Nazi death camps, but had the tragic misfortune to be in Budapest in January 1945 when the city fell to the Soviet army. Wallenberg was taken prisoner by the Russians and vanished into the Soviet prison system, never to be heard from again.

Retrace your steps to the park, where in the northeast corner is **Speakers' Corner** 35, a magnet for free speakers and pedagogues. It became a favourite place of protest in the 19th century and was officially recognised in 1872 as somewhere people could publicly state their opinions on Sundays, provided they weren't blasphemous, seditious or likely to incite violence. Speakers' Corner became famous – indeed, it became an institution – and huge crowds gathered to hear speakers, including such notable orators as Karl Marx and George Orwell.

Joy of Life Fountain

Continue south along the Broad Walk, which runs parallel to Park Lane, and just past the kiosk turn left to exit the park. On the central reservation, opposite Upper Brook Street, is one of London's most poignant memorials: David Backhouse's **Animals in War**

Food & Drink

2 **The Italian Gardens Café:** A handy spot to grab an alfresco coffee or breakfast before starting the walk (7.30/8am-4/7pm, depending on the time of year, £).

27 **Chucs Serpentine:** The stunning restaurant at the Serpentine Sackler Gallery is the perfect setting in which to enjoy contemporary Italian cuisine (9am-11pm, Sun 10.30pm, £-££).

47 **Rose & Crown:** Dating back over 400 years, this traditional pub is a good place to end your walk (11am-11pm, Sun noon-10.30pm, £).

Memorial 36, a tribute to the millions of animals that served, suffered and died alongside British, Commonwealth and Allied forces in the wars and conflicts of the 20th century. It features two heavily-laden mules trudging towards an opening between two swelling Portland stone screens, beyond which lies a grass mound with a cavorting horse and dog.

Return to the park, head left and some 400m further on you see Thomas Bayliss Huxley-Jones' exuberant **Joy of Life Fountain** 37, aka the Four Winds Fountain. Unveiled in 1963, it was donated by the Constance Fund – founded by the painter and art patron Sigismund Christian Hubert Goetze (1866-1939) and named after his wife – which encouraged art sculptures in London parks. The fountain features two bronze figures holding hands seeming to dance above the water, while four children emerge from the pool. Continue south along the Broad Walk for around 300m to arrive at the **7th July Memorial** 38, a short distance over to the left near Lovers Walk and the Curzon Gate. The memorial commemorates the victims of the London Bombings on 7th July 2005 – each of the 52 stainless steel pillars represents one of those killed in the atrocity.

To the right of the Broad Walk, almost parallel with the 7th July Memorial, is William Robert Colton's **Little Nell** 39, aka the Mermaid Fountain, installed in 1896 but stolen and replaced with today's concrete version in 1976. Heading south from Little Nell, you pass the bandstand on the right just before Serpentine Road, where (on the left) is the striking equestrian bronze **Cavalry Memorial** 40. Designed by Adrian Jones, the 1924 memorial commemorates the service of cavalry regiments in the World Wars. The sculpture depicts St George on horseback stepping over a defeated dragon, with a frieze of galloping horsemen around the base. Further south, on South Carriage Drive, there's a memorial to the Household Cavalry, commemorating four soldiers (and their horses) of the Blues and Royals regiment killed by an IRA bomb on 20th July 1982.

Little Nell

Achilles

Standing 18ft (5.5m) tall and made from cannons captured during the Duke of Wellington's campaigns in France, the naked Achilles – the Greek hero of the Trojan War – carries a sword and shield with his armour beside him, while his head is said to be modelled on that of the Duke of Wellington. Unveiled in 1822, it was the first statue installed in Hyde Park and was also London's first public nude statue; after much controversy, a fig leaf was added to cover Achilles' appendage (it isn't recorded whether this, too, was modelled on the Duke's).

Cross over Serpentine Road and enter the lovely Rose Garden, where there are two superb fountains. Lady Feodora Gleichen's beautiful **Huntress** 41 aka Diana/the Artemis Fountain, dates from 1899; it was made for the garden of Sir Walter Palmer's house in Berkshire and presented to Hyde Park by Lady Jean

Lord Byron

Palmer in 1906. Opposite is the charming **Boy and Dolphin** 42 by Alexander Munro (1863), featuring a pre-Raphaelite marble sculpture of a cherub and dolphin. From the fountains go east towards Hyde Park Corner, where over to the left is Richard Westmacott's imposing bronze of **Achilles** 43 (see box opposite).

Over to the right just outside the park – on the Achilles Way traffic island in Park Lane – is Richard Claude Belt's fine (1880) bronze of the poet **Lord Byron** 44 (1788-1824). The romantic poet is depicted with his beloved Newfoundland dog, Boatswain, seated on a 57-tonne plinth of pink and white marble presented by the Greek Government in 1882. Now marooned on a traffic island that's almost impossible to access, it seems an inappropriate spot for a romantic poet of Byron's stature.

Just south of Achilles is the **Queen Elizabeth Gate** 45, aka the Queen Mother's Gate, unveiled in 1993 to commemorate the 90th birthday of Queen Elizabeth, the Queen Mother. The gate's railings and lamps are by Giuseppe Lund and made of forged stainless steel and bronze, while the central screen is by David Wynne. Exit the park via the gates of Decimus Burton's (1828) **Hyde Park Screen** 46, which contain an elaborate frieze above the central arch by John Henning Snr and Jnr.

Just outside the Screen is the entrance to Hyde Park tube station. If you fancy some liquid refreshment after your exertions, you could try the historic **Rose & Crown** 47 pub at 2 Old Park Lane (off the north side of Piccadilly, just past the Hard Rock Café), once the living quarters for Oliver Cromwell's bodyguards.

Queen Elizabeth Gate

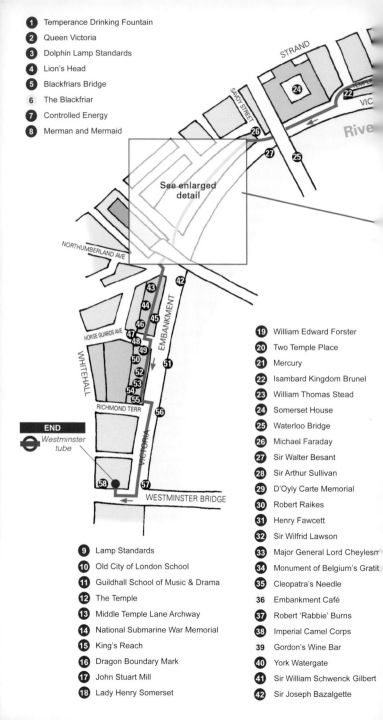

1 Temperance Drinking Fountain
2 Queen Victoria
3 Dolphin Lamp Standards
4 Lion's Head
5 Blackfriars Bridge
6 The Blackfriar
7 Controlled Energy
8 Merman and Mermaid

STRAND

SAVOY STREET

24

22

VIC

River

26

27

25

See enlarged detail

NORTHUMBERLAND AVE

43

42

44

EMBANKMENT

45

46

47

48

49

51

HORSE GUARDS AVE

50

52

53

54

55

WHITEHALL

RICHMOND TERR

56

END
Westminster tube

VICTORIA

58

57

WESTMINSTER BRIDGE

9 Lamp Standards
10 Old City of London School
11 Guildhall School of Music & Drama
12 The Temple
13 Middle Temple Lane Archway
14 National Submarine War Memorial
15 King's Reach
16 Dragon Boundary Mark
17 John Stuart Mill
18 Lady Henry Somerset

19 William Edward Forster
20 Two Temple Place
21 Mercury
22 Isambard Kingdom Brunel
23 William Thomas Stead
24 Somerset House
25 Waterloo Bridge
26 Michael Faraday
27 Sir Walter Besant
28 Sir Arthur Sullivan
29 D'Oyly Carte Memorial
30 Robert Raikes
31 Henry Fawcett
32 Sir Wilfrid Lawson
33 Major General Lord Cheylesm
34 Monument of Belgium's Gratit
35 Cleopatra's Needle
36 Embankment Café
37 Robert 'Rabbie' Burns
38 Imperial Camel Corps
39 Gordon's Wine Bar
40 York Watergate
41 Sir William Schwenck Gilbert
42 Sir Joseph Bazalgette

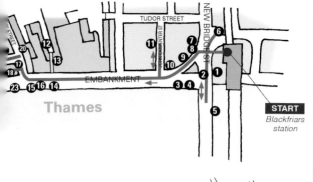

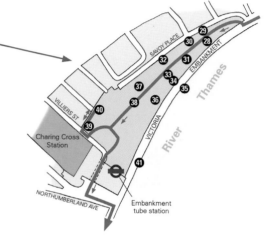

● Places of Interest   Food & Drink

Victoria Embankment

WALK 13

Distance: 2 miles (3¼ km)
Terrain: easy
Duration: 1-2 hours
Start: Blackfriars station
End: Westminster tube
Postcode: EC4R 2BB

VICTORIA EMBANKMENT

Walking east to west along the Victoria Embankment – from Blackfriars Bridge to Westminster Bridge – this stroll takes you through a wonderful chain of riverside gardens which was created as a by-product of the construction of London's sewerage system, a remarkable feat of Victorian engineering by Sir Joseph Bazalgette. During the excavation work, some 32 acres (13ha) of land was reclaimed and transformed into the new Embankment – and the series of gardens you see today.

We begin in Blackfriars, skirting the magnificent Inner and Middle Temples, before reaching Waterloo Bridge which commemorates Wellington's victory over Napoleon in 1815. Then we continue along the Embankment and through Victoria Embankment Gardens, passing landmarks such as the Savoy Hotel and Royal Horseguards Hotel, before finishing in the shadow of Big Ben.

Victoria Embankment

Victoria Embankment is one the richest sources of public art in London, home to some of its finest monuments, memorials and sculptures, from George Vulliamy's glorious lamp standards and Egyptian-style benches to Queen Boadicea and the dramatic Battle of Britain Memorial. This may be the shortest walk in the book but it take in over 50 works of art along its route.

Victoria Embankment

Start Walking…

We begin at Blackfriars Station, in an area of the City that takes its name from a 13th-century Dominican priory whose friars wore black habits. Leave the station via the Blackfriars Bridge exit (north) on New Bridge Street just before the bridge, where you see the charming but neglected **Temperance Drinking Fountain** ❶ sculpted by Wills Bros (1861) for the Coalbrookdale Iron Company. It depicts a girl in classical drapes, pouring water from an amphora – or at least it did when it functioned – and originally had three dolphins around the base. A few steps away on the traffic island just before the bridge is Charles Bell Birch's statue of **Queen Victoria** ❷, donated to the citizens of London by Sir Alfred Seale Haslam. The twice life-size bronze shows Victoria in full regalia with crown, sceptre and orb, mounted on a red granite plinth.

Down by the Thames you can spot the first of many **Dolphin Lamp Standards** ❸, designed by George John Vulliamy, architect to the Board of Works, and modelled by Charles Henry Mabey. Installed in the 1870s they're modelled on the statues of dolphins – the featured creatures are actually sturgeons –

with intertwined tails that decorate the Fontana del Nettuno in the Piazza del Popolo in Rome. Beneath the lamps on the river wall are bronze **Lion's Head** ❹ mooring rings, which were among the earliest elements installed in the Embankment's decorative scheme. For the tide to rise above the level of the lions' mouths would be a sign of severe flooding, which gave rise to the saying: 'if the lions drink, London will sink'.

Blackfriars Bridge ❺ was constructed by distinguished builder and architect Thomas Cubitt and opened in 1869, replacing an earlier structure from the 1760s. On the bridge's piers are stone carvings of water birds by John Birnie Philip; on

Victoria Embankment Gardens

The gardens opened in 1874 and extend to 11 acres (4.5ha) in total, stretching along the north side of the Thames between Middle Temple Gardens and Westminster Bridge. They were designed by Alexander McKenzie and created in four sections: the Temple Garden to the northeast, the Main Gardens in the middle following the bend of the Thames, and two sections – Whitehall Gardens and the Ministry of Defence – to the south.

The Blackfriar

Built in 1875, this narrow, wedge-shaped tavern is tucked up against the railway lines at Blackfriars. The pub's name on the façade – decorated by Henry Poole in 1903 – is displayed in mosaic tiles, and a statue of a laughing friar stands above the main door. However, it's the interior that makes the pub truly extraordinary. It was remodelled from 1904 onwards, with sculptors Nathaniel Hitch, Frederick Thomas Callcott and Henry Poole all contributing, and every interior surface decorated – in marble, mosaic, bas-reliefs and sculptures – while the walls are decorated with illustrations of jolly monks; some are singing and playing instruments or picking apples and grapes, while others gather fish and eels for their meatless days and another boils an egg. The overall impression is decidedly ecclesiastical in design, with a strong Art Nouveau character.

your steps past the station to Queen Victoria Street, where on the north side is **The Blackfriar** 6 (see box), London's most ornate pub and deservedly Grade II listed, which is a good spot for breakfast or a brew.

Old City of London School

Opposite Blackfriars Station, at the start of the Victoria Embankment, stands Unilever House, an imposing Neoclassical Art Deco office building with an enormous curved frontage. It was designed by James Lomax-Simpson and Sir John James Burnet & Partners and constructed 1929-1933. The entrances at the corners of the building are surmounted by large plinths on which stand Sir William Reid Dick's sculptures of human figures restraining horses, called **Controlled Energy** 7. There are also **Merman and Mermaid** 8 keystone figures by Gilbert Ledward over the same entrance doors. To the side of the main entrance are Walter Gilbert's handsome bronze **Lamp Standards** 9, decorated with relief panels.

the eastern (downstream) side the carvings portray marine life and seabirds, while those on the western (upstream) side depict freshwater birds. The bridge achieved notoriety in 1982 when the body of Robert Calvi, a former chairman of Italy's largest private bank, was found hanging from one of its arches, courtesy of the Mafia. From the bridge, retrace

Continuing past Unilever House, the next building along is the beautiful **Old**

The Blackfriar

City of London School ⑩; the school moved to Queen Victoria Street (near St Paul's) in 1986 and the building is now occupied by bankers J. P. Morgan. Dating from 1883, it's designed in Italian Renaissance style by Davis and Emanuel and incorporates a wealth of sculptures, including full-sized statues (by John Daymond & Son) of Francis Bacon, John Milton, Isaac Newton and William Shakespeare on its façade, with Thomas More around the left side. There are also pairs of allegorical girls, illustrating the different subjects of study. Just past the school, on the corner of John Carpenter Street, is the distinctive Gothic red-brick Sion College, designed by Arthur Blomfield in 1886. A short way along on the left in John Carpenter Street is the former **Guildhall School of Music & Drama** ⑪, designed by Sir Horace Jones; a highly decorated palazzo stone building, it contains commemorative panels to composers and musicians Tallis, Gibbons, Purcell, Arne and Sterndale Bennett, along with musical and floral décor.

Carry on along the Victoria Embankment, where after a few hundred metres you come to the **Temple** ⑫, home to the Inner and Middle Temples, two of London's four Inns of Court dating back to the 14th century. Visitors are welcome at the Temple but there's no public right of way, the external gates are locked at weekends, on public holidays and at night – and there's no access to buildings (including Middle Temple Hall) unless authorised or part of a tour.

Middle Temple Lane Archway

The grand entrance to the Middle Temple was designed by Edward Middleton Barry in the late 1870s, with sculptural work by William Calder Marshall and decoration by Mabey & Co. It features two full figures – Justice on the left and Learning on the right – in canopied niches, various half figures higher up and little heads in roundels. Above the entrance is a shield with a portrait of Queen Victoria held by two cherubs with wings and fishtails. The courtyard side of the archway is much plainer than that facing the gardens, and features shields showing Pegasus, emblem of the Inner Temple, on the left, and the lamb and flag representing the Middle Temple on the right.

However, you can explore Temple Gardens (restricted opening hours) via Middle Temple Lane and the glorious **Middle Temple Lane Archway** ⑬ (see box).

Middle Temple Hall & Gardens

Walk 13

Food & Drink

(6) The Blackfriar: Historic Nicholson's pub, serving food (including breakfast) and ales in an ecclesiastical atmosphere (10am-11pm, Sat 9am-11pm, Sun noon-10.30pm, £).

(36) Embankment Café: A peaceful spot for coffee or lunch, with a charming garden pavilion (8am-6pm, Sat-Sun 9am, £).

(39) Gordon's Wine Bar: Established in 1890, Gordon's is the city's oldest wine bar with a vast list of wines and interesting cheeses (11am-11pm, Sun noon-10pm, £).

(58) St Stephen's Tavern: A magnificent Victorian tavern popular with political types, serving fine ales and pub grub (10am-11.30pm, Sun 10.30pm, £).

Submariners Memorial

commemorating Royal Navy submariners who died in the two World Wars. Unveiled in 1922, the memorial was built into a granite pier that formed part of the entrance to Temple Pier. Two large plaques on the sides list the 132 submarines lost in the wars, the First World War on the left and the Second on the right. The bronze relief by Frederick Brook Hitch depicts, in cross section, the interior of a submarine in which sailors carried out their work in cramped and claustrophobic conditions. On either side, sea creatures in human form surround the vessel with nets and seaweed. Just past the submariners' memorial is Charles Doman's (1936) **King's Reach Memorial 15**, tucked beneath Temple Stairs Arch – part of Joseph Bazalgette's design for the Embankment in 1868 – and featuring cherubs on ships' prows. The memorial marks the naming of the Thames between London Bridge and Westminster Bridge as King's Reach, in honour of the 25th anniversary of the accession of George V.

Return to the Victoria Embankment and cross to the embankment wall to see Arthur Heron Ryan Tenison's **National Submarine War Memorial 14**,

A few metres east of the memorial is a City of London **Dragon Boundary Mark** **16** (right), a cast iron statue of a dragon on a

stone plinth, one of a pair (the other is on the opposite side of the road) which mark the boundary of the City of London. The dragons are painted silver, with details on their wings and tongues picked out in red, and hold shields bearing the City of London coat of arms.

Cross back to the northern side of Victoria Embankment and continue west to the first section of Victoria Embankment Gardens (Mon-Sat 7.30am to dusk – see box, page 151), called the Temple Garden. At the eastern end of the garden is Thomas Woolner's (1878) seated bronze statue of **John Stuart Mill** **17** (1806-1873), philosopher, political economist and civil servant, dubbed 'the most influential English-speaking philosopher of the 19th century'. A short distance away on the embankment side of the garden is George Edward Wade's charming memorial fountain commemorating **Lady Henry Somerset** **18** (1851-1921), depicting a young girl with a bowl representing Temperance (a Victorian virtue based on moderation and, often, abstinence from alcohol). The wife of Lord Henry Somerset (8th Duke of Beaufort), Lady Somerset was a philanthropist, temperance leader and campaigner for women's

rights. Near the end of the garden on the right is Henry Richard Hope-Pinker's bronze of **William Edward Forster** **19** (1818-1886), a British industrialist, philanthropist and Liberal Party statesman. A self-made man, Forster began his career in the woollen industry working 12 hours a day, and is credited with the creation of a national system of primary-school education.

Opposite Temple Garden on the embankment wall is George Frampton's (1913) plaque in memory of **William Thomas Stead** **23** (1849-1912), a renowned English newspaper editor and pioneer of investigative journalism, who went down with the *Titanic*. Just behind the garden is **Two Temple Place** **20** (see box, page 156), a Gothic Revival extravaganza and treasure house. Next door is Postmodern Globe House, which retains two life-size bronzes of **Mercury** **21** by Sir Charles Wheeler on either side of the entrance, dating from 1933 and retained from Electra House which once stood on this site. From Two Temple Place, follow

Lady Henry Somerset

the road west to the end, where there's a fine statue of Victorian engineer **Isambard Kingdom Brunel** **22** (1806-1859) by Carlo Marochetti, with a surround by Richard Norman Shaw. Considered by many to be England's finest engineer, Brunel is depicted wearing a frock coat, and stands in a relaxed pose with a quizzically raised eyebrow.

Continuing along Victoria Embankment you pass **Somerset House** 24 (see **Walk 7**), a spectacular 18th-century Neoclassical building designed by William Chambers (1723-1796), housing the excellent Courtauld

Michael Faraday

Gallery. The Somerset House pediment on the river frontage was designed by Richard Rathbone in the 18th century. Opposite the house is the RNLI Thames Lifeboat Station, originally built to rescue would-be suicides jumping off **Waterloo Bridge** 25 . Just past the bridge in Savoy Place, is an impressive statue of **Michael Faraday** 26 (1791-1867), the renowned British scientist whose discoveries include the principles underlying electromagnetic induction, diamagnetism and electrolysis. The statue – outside the Institution of Engineering and Technology – is a bronze copy of a marble original at the Royal Institution, sculpted by John Henry Foley in 1874. Opposite Faraday on the embankment wall is George Frampton's 1902 bronze relief commemorating **Sir Walter Besant** 27 (1836-1901), novelist, historian and founder of the Society of Authors.

Just past Savoy Place is the main section of Victoria Embankment Gardens (once called the Adelphi Gardens), where there's a café and bandstand, and a wealth of monuments and statues. Soon after entering the gardens, on the left is a beautiful statue by William Goscombe John (1902) of **Sir Arthur Sullivan** 28 (1842-1900), the composer half of the Gilbert and Sullivan duo famous

---

Two Temple Place

Built in 1895 for William Waldorf Astor (1848-1919) on reclaimed land following completion of the Victoria Embankment, Two Temple Place was designed by John Loughborough Pearson and his son Frank. It's both an architectural gem and a treasure house of exquisite works by leading artists of the day. It has splendid carvings on the exterior stonework by Nathaniel Hitch and above the parapets is John Starkie Gardner's superb gilded weathervane in beaten copper, depicting Columbus' caravel *Santa Maria*. The enchanting bronze lamp standards flanking the base of the entrance steps are a foretaste of the riches within. (For opening hours and exhibitions, see https://twotempleplace.org.)

Victoria Embankment

or their comic operas – W. S. Gilbert has his own memorial just past Embankment Pier (see below). The delightful mourning girl (an allegorical figure of Music) collapsing against the stele below Sullivan's bust is an outstanding example of Art Nouveau design. Almost opposite Sullivan, outside the Savoy Hotel's riverside entrance, is the **D'Oyly Carte Memorial** ㉙ , in the form of an equatorial armillary sphere, installed in 1989 to commemorate the hotel's centenary.

Sir Arthur Sullivan

The next three statues along are Thomas Brock's bronze of **Robert Raikes** ㉚ (1736-1811) on the right, English philanthropist and Anglican layman, credited as the founder of Sunday schools; on the left is Mary Grant and Sir George Frampton's (1886) monument to the blind **Henry Fawcett** ㉛ (1833-1884), British academic, statesman, Postmaster General and economist, and (on

the right) David McGill's 1909 bronze of **Sir Wilfrid Lawson** ㉜ (1829-1906). Lawson was an English temperance campaigner and radical, anti-imperialist Liberal Party politician – and reportedly the leading humorist in the House of Commons.

Just past Lawson's statue, on the left-hand side, is Edwin Lutyens' 1930 memorial to **Herbert Francis Eaton, 3rd Baron Cheylesmore** ㉝ (1848-1925). Soldier, administrator and philanthropist, Cheylesmore was chairman of London County Council and presided over courts martial during the First World War. Made of Portland stone, the memorial contains seats backing on to a decorative screen facing a small pond. Behind the memorial, back on the Victoria Embankment (you need to leave the gardens to view it), is Sir Reginald Blomfield's **Monument of Belgium's Gratitude** ㉞ . The central bronze sculpture by Victor Rousseau depicts a woman accompanied by a boy and girl with garlands of flowers. To each side of the bronze are seated limestone relief figures representing Justice and Honour. The 1920 monument was a gift from Belgium in gratitude for Britain's assistance in the First World War and for sheltering Belgian refugees – including Rousseau – who fled the war. Opposite the monument on the river embankment is **Cleopatra's Needle** ㉟ (see box, page 158).

Returning to the gardens and continuing southwest, you pass the **Embankment Café** 36 on the left, while on the right is John

157

Cleopatra's Needle

An obelisk dating from around 1450BC and the Egyptian city of Heliopolis, Cleopatra's Needle was a gift from the ruler of Egypt, erected here in 1877. It's flanked by two faux-Egyptian bronze sphinxes, designed by George John Vulliamy and modelled by Charles Henry Mabey. Vulliamy and Mabey also designed the handsome, Egyptian-themed benches – featuring either sphinxes or camels – dotted along the embankment (and the dolphin lamp standards that you saw earlier).

Steel's fine statue of Scots poet **Robert 'Rabbie' Burns** ③⑦ (1759-1796), regarded as the national poet of Scotland. Just past Burns in the centre of the path is an elegant memorial to the **Imperial Camel Corps** ③⑧ by Major Cecil Brown, who served in the Corps. The smaller than life-size bronze depicts a soldier riding a camel, mounted on a Portland stone pedestal bearing bronze panels on its four sides. The memorial commemorates soldiers from Australia, India, New Zealand and the UK who died in Middle East campaigns during the First World War. Behind the gardens is the '30s Art Deco New Adelphi building, with four large relief stone figures at the corners by Gilbert Ledward and others. If you fancy a drink or lunch the **Embankment Café** 36 that you

passed earlier is a nice spot for an alfresco break or, if you prefer something stronger, you could try **Gordon's Wine Bar** 39 in Villiers Street at the rear of the gardens just past the **York Watergate** ④⓪ (see box opposite).

Cross the road just before Embankment tube station to see Sir George Frampton's (1915) memorial to **Sir William Schwenck Gilbert** ④① (1836-1911) on the retaining river wall on the north side of Hungerford Bridge. The bronze contains a portrait relief of Sir Arthur Sullivan's lyrical partner with figures of Tragedy and Comedy on either side; tragedy has a book on her lap and is handing Gilbert flowers, whilst Comedy holds puppet characters from *The Mikado*. Just beyond the Hungerford and Golden Jubilee foot bridges on the river wall is George Simmons' memorial to **Sir Joseph Bazalgette** ④② (1819-1891), the eminent Victorian engineer who built London's sewer network and the Victoria Embankment; above the bronze bust is the Latin inscription: *Flumini vincula posuit* (he chained the river).

Imperial Camel Corps

Victoria Embankment

Cross over the Victoria Embankment to Whitehall Gardens, just west of Northumberland Avenue, in the shadow of the splendid (Grade I listed) Royal Horseguards Hotel, constructed in 1884 and modelled on a French chateau. The first statue you see is Matthew Noble's 1871 bronze of **Lieutenant-General James Outram** ㊸ (1803-1863). A much-decorated English general, Outram fought in the First Anglo-Afghan war, the Anglo-Persian War and the Indian Rebellion of 1857. In the middle of the gardens is Thomas Brock's statue of **Sir Henry Bartle Frere** ㊹ (1815-1884) erected in 1887. A British colonial administrator, Frere's reckless actions as High Commissioner for southern Africa led to the First Boer War and earned him an official censure

(but didn't stop them putting up a statue to him…). A bit further along on the Embankment – just outside the gardens – is a striking memorial to **Samuel Plimsoll** ㊺ by Ferdinand Victor Blundstone. Plimsoll devised the line on a ship's hull that shows its maximum safe draft and earned him the sobriquet, 'the sailor's friend'. Before leaving this section of gardens you come to Joseph Edgar Boehm's magnificent 1884 statue of **Sir William Tyndale** ㊻ (1494-1536, see box, page 160).

Leaving Whitehall Gardens cross Horse Guards Avenue to the final section of Victoria Embankment Gardens, known as the Ministry of Defence section as it's dominated by the vast MoD building at its rear. On the right just after entering the gardens are the remains of the old Whitehall Steps to the Thames, also known as the **Queen Mary Steps** ㊼ – built for Mary II in 1691 by Sir Christopher Wren – together with the early 16th-century Thames Embankment wall. Discovered in 1939, they're the only existing remains of Whitehall Palace, the residence of Tudor monarchs. Nearby is William Hamo Thorneycroft's

Samuel Plimsoll

York Watergate

An intriguing reminder of a time when a string of mansions lined the Strand and backed onto the Thames, the York Watergate by architect Balthazar Gerbier is all that remains of York House (as it later became), built as a London base for the Bishops of Norwich, probably in the 1230s. The Watergate was built around 1625 for the Duke of Buckingham, but now sits 150m back from the river – a stark illustration of just how much land was reclaimed by the construction of the Thames Embankment

Walk 13

fine statue of **General Charles George Gordon** **48** (1833-1885), aka 'Gordon of Khartoum'. Gordon saw action in the Crimea and made his reputation in China, although he's best known for his stand in Khartoum, where he died after almost a year of defending the city, which fell to the Mahdi's forces just two days before reinforcements arrived.

The next statue you come to is that of Marshal of the Royal Air Force **Viscount Portal** **49** (1893-1971) by Oscar Nemon, unveiled in 1975. Portal served as a bomber pilot in the First World

War and rose to become Chief of the Air Staff in the Second World War. Just past Viscount Portal is the **Fleet Air Arm Memorial** **50**, aka Daedalus, by James Butler, dating from 2000. The figure of Daedalus – atop a column rising out of a plinth reminiscent of the prow of a ship – as a modern pilot reflects on his fallen comrades. Opposite Daedalus on the Embankment is William Reid Dick's **Royal Air Force Memorial** **51**, from 1923, topped with a golden eagle. Returning to the gardens, you come to Philip Jackson's **Korean War Memorial** **52**, a gift from the Republic of Korea in 2014. It shows a British soldier standing in quiet contemplation in front of a Portland stone obelisk on a base of Welsh slate. This is followed by William McMillan's 1961 statue of another Marshal of the Royal Air Force, **Viscount Trenchard** **53** (1873-1956). Trenchard was the driving force behind the creation of the RAF in 1918, and is considered the 'father of the Royal Air Force'.

Towards the southern end of the gardens is Paul Day's **Iraq & Afghanistan Memorial** **54**, commemorating Britons who served in the Gulf, Afghanistan and Iraq Wars between 1990 and 2015, and unveiled by Queen Elizabeth in 2017. The final memorial is Frank Forster's **Chindit**

Korean War Memorial

Memorial **55** from 1990, crowned with a bronze *Chinthe* or Burmese temple guardian – the mythical beast from which the Chindit special forces took their name. Medallions to the front and rear depict the force's badge and include a portrait (at the rear) of their founder, Major General Orde Wingate (1903-1944). Wingate was killed in an aircraft accident and is buried in Arlington National Cemetery in Virginia, USA.

The most dramatic war memorial of all isn't in the gardens, but on Victoria Embankment opposite Richmond Terrace and New Scotland Yard: the magnificent **Battle of Britain Memorial 56** (see box).

From the memorial, continue south past Westminster Pier where, on a pedestal to the right of the steps just before Westminster Bridge, is Thomas and William Hamo Thorneycroft's spectacular

Queen Boadicea

bronze of **Queen Boadicea 57** and her daughters driving a war chariot. Boadicea (Boudicca), queen of the Celtic Iceni tribe, led an unsuccessful uprising against the occupying forces of the Roman Empire in around AD60. She died in a battle shortly afterwards, although how she died and the place of her defeat is unknown. Today, she's a British folk hero.

Cross the road to Westminster tube station which marks the end of the walk. If you fancy a drink or lunch, **St Stephen's Tavern 58** is just past the station. Built in 1873, it's now owned by Dorset brewers Hall & Woodhouse and has been restored to its former Victorian glory.

Battle of Britain Memorial

Installed in 2005 on the 65th anniversary of the battle – which took place between July and October 1940 – the memorial's centrepiece 'scramble' depicts airmen running to their planes to intercept enemy aircraft. Conceived by Bill Bond and sculpted by Paul Day, it's engraved with all 2,936 names of the British and allied airmen who fought in the battle (544 died in the battle and another 795 didn't survive the war). Britain's victory in the battle saved the country from invasion and ultimately cost Germany the war.

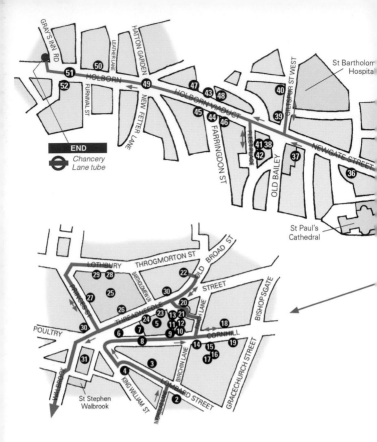

1. The Monument
2. Chimera with Personifications of Fire and the Sea
3. Golden Grasshopper
4. Electricity and Speed
5. Royal Exchange
6. Duke of Wellington
7. London Troops War Memorial
8. James Henry Greathead
9. Cornhill Water Pump
10. Cornhill Fountain
11. Sir Thomas Gresham
12. Paul Julius Reuter
13. President Abraham Lincoln
14. Thomas Gray
15. St Michael, Cornhill
16. St Michael Cornhill War Memorial
17. Tympanum
18. Gargoyle Beasts
19. Counting House
20. La Maternité
21. George Peabody
22. City Wing
23. Sir Hugh Myddleton
24. Richard Whittington
25. Bank of England
26. Lady of the Bank
27. Ariel
28. The Lothbury Ladies
29. Sir John Soane
30. National Westminster Bank

Monument to Chancery Lane

WALK 14

Distance: 3 miles (5 km)

Terrain: easy

Duration: 1½-2½ hours

Start: Monument tube

End: Chancery Lane tube

Postcode: EC4R 9AA

MONUMENT TO CHANCERY LANE

This walk begins at the Monument, built to commemorate the Great Fire of London, and heads north to the area around the Bank of England in the heart of the 'City', the historic nucleus of London. The streets flanking the Royal Exchange and the Bank are rich in public art – statues, busts, memorials and commemorative plaques – to the great and good. In fact, around almost every corner in the City you'll find a striking work of art or a memorial to some historic character or deed, along with a wealth of beautiful buildings (see also Walk 15).

From the financial district we detour to Cannon Street and the ancient ward of Cordwainer, before heading west on Cheapside and Newgate Street, passing St Paul's (see Walk 7), the London Stock Exchange and the Central Criminal Court ('Old Bailey'). We continue west to Holborn and the historic ward of Farringdon – split into Farringdon Within and Farringdon Without in 1394 – denoting whether the area was inside or outside the London Wall. The walk terminates in Chancery Lane which forms the western boundary of the City.

Sculpture in the City

Since 2010, the critically acclaimed 'Sculpture in the City' has been staged in the City of London with a public display of contemporary works from internationally renowned artists. For information see www.cityoflondon.gov.uk/things-to-do/visit-the-city/whats-on/pages/sculpture-in-the-city.aspx.

Monument to Chancery Lane

Start Walking...

Exit Monument tube station, named after **The Monument to the Great Fire of London** ❶ (see box), to give it its full name, that destroyed most of the City in 1666. Go right along Eastcheap and right again down Fish Street Hill to the Monument, which stands on the left at the junction with Monument Street. Turn right along Monument Street and right again down King William Street to return to the tube station.

Cross to the north side of Cannon Street and walk along King William Street and take the second right on Nicholas Lane which leads to Lombard Street. Turn right to see Francis William Doyle-Jones' **Chimera with Personifications of Fire and the Sea** ❷ above the entrance to 24-28 Lombard Street (the old Royal Insurance Buildings). This group of three topless ladies symbolically depicts the power of the Sea on the left, Fire on the right and, in the centre, a semi-sphinx with wings representing the uncertainty of the future (pessimistic lot, insurers!). Go left along Lombard Street, where on the right is a **Golden Grasshopper** ❸ outside number 68, the site of the former home of Sir Thomas Gresham

The Monument

At 202ft (61m) the Monument is the world's tallest isolated stone column, designed by Sir Christopher Wren and scientist Dr Robert Hooke, and built between 1671 and 1677. On the west panel of the pedestal is Caius Gabriel Cibber's beautiful allegorical relief, which portrays Charles II 'affording protection to the desolate City and freedom to its rebuilders and inhabitants'. You can climb to the top (fee) and enjoy a bird's-eye view of the City (see www.themonument.info for opening times).

(1519-79), founder of the Royal Exchange. The grasshopper was Gresham's heraldic symbol and there are a few dotted around the area.

At the end of Lombard Street turn left into King William Street and just past St Mary Woolnoth on the left is Oliver Wheatley's (1899) **Electricity and Speed** ❹; the former is represented by a female figure sparking a flash of electricity with her pointed finger, the latter by Mercury. Return to Lombard Street and head north to the crossroads, aka the Bank junction, then right along Cornhill. Immediately on the left is the **Royal Exchange** ❺ building (see box, page 166), which has a superb pediment sculpture by Richard Westmacott Jr incorporating 17 figures of merchants and traders. In 2001, the building was refurbished and became a luxury shopping centre.

Golden Grasshopper

You can get a taste of its former glory by stopping for a coffee at the Grand Café **5** .

Royal Exchange

The first Royal Exchange was founded by Sir Thomas Gresham, merchant and advisor to Elizabeth I, as a centre of commerce for the City of London, and opened in 1571. It was destroyed in the Great Fire and a subsequent building was also gutted by fire. Today's (third) Royal Exchange was designed by Sir William Tite and opened by Queen Victoria in 1844. In 1892, 24 large panel paintings (by various artists) were installed on the first floor walls, depicting British history and trade from its earliest times. As a nod to its founder, the Gresham family crest of a grasshopper can still be seen on the building's weathervane.

In front of the Exchange overlooking Bank junction is Francis Leggatt Chantrey's bronze equestrian statue of the **Duke of Wellington 6**, completed by Henry Weekes in 1844 after Chantrey's death three years earlier. Directly in front of the Royal Exchange is Sir Aston Webb's **London Troops War Memorial 7** commemorating Londoners who fought in the two World Wars. The striking 25ft (7.5m) high Portland stone memorial incorporates three bronzes by Alfred Drury: two life-size soldiers – one representing the Royal Fusiliers, the other the Royal Field Artillery – plus a lion rampant bearing a medallion of St George and the Dragon on top of the column. Opposite the war memorial on a traffic island in Cornhill is James Butler's statue of **James Henry Greathead 8**, erected in 1994. Greathead (1844-1896) was a South African civil engineer who's best known as chief engineer of the City & South London Railway (forerunner of the London Underground).

Head east along Cornhill – note the handsome clock on the corner of the Royal Exchange, the twin of one on the opposite side – and cross over to number 32, the old Cornhill Insurance building, where the door has some lovely carved panels dating from 1939. Back on the left-hand side, near the end of the Royal Exchange building, is the **Cornhill Water Pump 9** dating from 1799. Go left past the pump, where in the middle of the Royal Exchange pedestrian piazza, is Stephen R. Melton's **Cornhill Fountain 10**, erected by the Metropolitan Drinking Fountain and Cattle Trough Association in 1911. Just past the fountain,

high above the eastern entrance of the Royal Exchange (in a niche on the tower) is William Behnes' 1845 statue of **Sir Thomas Gresham 11**. Back on

Paul Julius Reuter

St Michael, Cornhill

A medieval parish church stood here from 1133 but was lost in the Great Fire, and replaced in the 17th century by the present building, attributed to Sir Christopher Wren and Nicholas Hawksmoor. The building (Grade I listed) was further embellished by Sir George Gilbert Scott and Herbert Williams in the 19th century, and is one of the City's most beautiful churches with some splendid stained glass.

ground level is Michael Black's large granite herm (bust on a pillar) from 1976, portraying German-born **Paul Julius Reuter** **12** (1816-1899), pioneer of telegraphy and the founder of Reuters News Agency. Inside the foyer at the eastern entrance is Andrew O'Connor's bust of **President Abraham Lincoln 13** (1809-1865).

Return to Cornhill, where a short way along on the right on the Zenith Bank building (number 39) is Frederick William Pomeroy's memorial plaque to poet **Thomas Gray 14** (1716-1771), who lived in a house on this spot. Just past St Michael's Alley is the church of **St Michael, Cornhill 15** (see box), where to the right of the entrance stands Richard Reginald Goulden's outstanding **St Michael Cornhill War Memorial 16**, commemorating 2,130 men from the parish who served in the First World War. The statue depicts the Archangel Michael with wings erect, wearing Roman segmented armour and a helmet, holding aloft a flaming sword. By the angel's right foot are two lions, one biting the other, representing war, while by the left foot are four cherubs looking upwards, representing peace. Above the church entrance is John Birnie Philip's (1860) beautiful high relief **Tympanum 17**, portraying St Michael disputing with Satan. Almost opposite the church, the red terracotta building next to Newman's Court has two Gothic **Gargoyle Beasts 18**, by William James Neatby, perched high up on the façade, while just past St Michael's is the **Counting House 19**, a Fuller's pub occupying a stunning former banking hall.

Retrace your steps west along Cornhill, turn right down Finch Lane and duck left along Royal Exchange Avenue. At the end, where it opens onto the Royal Exchange piazza, you find the lovely **La Maternité 20**, aka Charity; a grey and pink granite fountain by Aimé-Jules Dalou dating from 1878, it incorporates a bronze statue of a mother with two children, one at her breast. Almost opposite is William Wetmore Story's 1868 bronze of **George Peabody 21** (1795-1869), an American-British financier widely regarded as the 'father of modern philanthropy'. At the end of Royal Exchange

La Maternité

City Wing

go right on Threadneedle Street and left down Old Broad Street, where at the entrance to Threadneedle Walk on the left is Christopher Le Brun's modern sculpture, **City Wing** ㉒ , a 33-ft (10m) bronze of a bird's wing unveiled in 2013. Return to Threadneedle Street, where opposite, on the Royal Exchange building, are two stone statues in niches. On the left is Samuel Joseph's **Sir Hugh Myddleton** ㉓ (1560-1631), the driving force behind the New River project which brought fresh water to the City, while on the right is

John Carew's statue of **Richard 'Dick' Whittington** ㉔ (1354-1423), four times Lord Mayor of London.

Opposite the Royal Exchange is the **Bank of England** ㉕ (see box), dubbed 'the Old Lady of Threadneedle Street'. The remodelled building is adorned with sculptures by Sir Charles Wheeler circa 1930, which include the **Lady of the Bank** ㉖ in the centre of the pediment above the Threadneedle Street entrance. Also by Wheeler are six giant figures on the frontage above the lower balustrade – four male telamones (a figure used as a pillar to support an entablature or other structure) on the outside and two inner female caryatids (similar to telamones, but female figures). Continue along Threadneedle Street and go right down Princes Street, where midway along is Wheeler's gilded bronze figure on the cupola of Tivoli Corner, dubbed **Ariel** ㉗ but correctly titled the 'Spirit of the Winds'. At the end of Princes Street, go right into Lothbury to see more of Wheeler's work: four stone female figures from 1937, known as the **Lothbury Ladies** ㉘ , high up on the frontage of the bank. Tucked into the west niche at ground level is William Reid Dick's statue of **Sir John Soane** ㉙ (1753-1837); Soane was the original architect of the Bank building and this is a

---

Bank of England

The central bank of the United Kingdom, the Bank of England was established in 1694. The original building was designed by Sir John Soane in the 18th-19th centuries, but was controversially rebuilt by Sir Herbert Baker in the '20s and '30s, demolishing most of Soane's building in the process. This act was described by architectural historian Nikolaus Pevsner as 'the greatest architectural crime in the City of London of the 20th century'. Nevertheless, the façade has some excellent sculptures – and there's also an interesting free museum (see www.bankofengland.co.uk/museum).

Mansion House

A rare surviving grand Georgian Palladian palace, built between 1739 and 1752 by George Dance the Elder, the Mansion House contains the Lord Mayor's private office and is a centre for meetings, conferences, banquets and entertaining. Its magnificent rooms are the venue for a number of the City's grandest official functions, including an annual dinner at which the Chancellor of the Exchequer gives his Mansion House Speech regarding the British economy. The cellars formerly contained cells, where the suffragette Emmeline Pankhurst was once held prisoner.

somewhat dubious honour given how his masterpiece was defaced.

Return to the Bank junction, where on the corner of Princes Street, Poultry and Mansion House Street is the **National Westminster Bank** ㉚ , designed by Sir Edwin Cooper and built 1929-1932. In the ground floor alcoves are two pairs of classical allegorical figures by Charles Doman, symbolising financial virtues; the figures on the Princes Street façade represent Security and Prosperity, while those on the south façade represent Courage and Integrity. High above on the corner parapet is Ernest Gillick's allegorical group of a seated Britannia flanked by the figures of Higher and Lower Mathematics with Mercury, Truth and the Owl of Wisdom.

Opposite the bank is **Mansion House** ㉛ (see box), the official residence of the Lord Mayor of the City of London. The Lord Mayor is

Food & Drink

⑤ **Grand Café:** Located in the courtyard of the Royal Exchange, the Grand Café opens from breakfast to dinner; it's relatively expensive but worth it just to admire the glorious building (Mon-Fri 8am-10pm, £-££).

⑲ **The Counting House:** Pub located in a gorgeous 19th-century banking hall, with a splendid glass domed ceiling (Mon-Fri 10am-11pm, £).

㉞ **Bow Wine Vaults Bar:** Smart wine bar/brasserie with outside tables, plus British/Mediterranean cuisine in the vaults (020-7248 1121, Mon-Fri 11am-11pm, £-££).

(52) **Caffè Vergnano:** Elegant Italian café serving excellent coffee and pastries (Mon-Fri 7am-7pm, Sat 8.30am-5.30pm, Sun 9am-5.30pm, £).

elected for one year, the position being unpaid and apolitical, not to be confused with the Mayor of London which is a paid, elected, political position with a four-year term.

Old Bailey

Atop the court's dome is one of London's most iconic statues: Frederick William Pomeroy's (1906) gilded bronze figure of Lady Justice, a powerfully-built woman, arms outstretched, holding her symbols of sword and the scales of justice. Pomeroy also created the trio of Fortitude and Truth flanking the Recording Angel over the old main entrance. The frieze (relief panels) above the recessed centre bay on the main façade is by Alfred Turner, while there's more outstanding sculpture inside the building.

From Mansion House, go left down Walbrook to Cannon Street, where opposite the station is Stephen Melton's 1997 bronze of a **LIFFE Trader 32 ,** which stands for London International Financial Futures Exchange. Go west along Cannon Street and turn right into Queen Street, cross Queen Victoria Street and then go left on Watling Street. A short distance up on the left is Alma Boyes' superb **Cordwainer 33** statue, a bronze of a shoemaker, installed in 2002 to

celebrate the centenary of the Cordwainers Club. Cordwainers were professional shoemakers who lived and worked here, in the Ward of Cordwainer, the centre for shoemaking in medieval times. The trade has its own livery company: the Worshipful Company of Cordwainers.

Continue along Watling Street and go right on Bow Lane, then left into Bow Churchyard alleyway just past the **Bow Wine Vaults Bar 34** , a popular lunch venue. In the middle of the Churchyard, adjoining the church of St Mary-le-Bow (rebuilt by Sir Christopher Wren after the Great Fire), is a statue of local citizen **Captain John Smith 35** (1580-1631), a cordwainer by trade. Smith founded the first permanent English settlement in America in 1606 –

at Jamestown, Virginia – where Pocahontas, the daughter of an Indian chief, allegedly saved his life. The statue is a Charles Renick (1960) copy of the original by William Couper in 1907, presented to the Corporation of London by the Jamestown Foundation of the Commonwealth of Virginia. At the end of Bow Churchyard go left

Cordwalner

Monument to Chancery Lane

London Stock Exchange

on Cheapside ('market place' in old English), passing One New Change, the City's only major shopping centre, and St Paul's Cathedral (see **Walk 7**) on your left.

At the end of Cheapside continue along Newgate Street, the site of one of the historic seven gates of the London Wall around the City, dating back to Roman times. From the 12th century (at least) this was the location of the infamous Newgate Prison for debtors and felons. A short way down Newgate Street, on the left is the **London Stock Exchange 36**, the third-largest stock exchange in the world, while on the right is Christchurch Greyfriars Church Garden. Around 100m past the garden (on the left) is the Edwardian Baroque Central

Criminal Court – commonly known as the **Old Bailey 37** (see box opposite) after the street where it's located – where major criminal cases are tried.

Opposite is Britannia House (16-17 Old Bailey), which has a pair of fine figures above the entrance portico, the **Progress of Communication 38** (sculptor unknown), representing rail and sea travel (the building was built for the Chatham and Dover Railway Company). The female figure on the left holds a steam train

Charles Lamb

in her hand, while the male on the right rests his hands on an anchor and the prow of a ship. Return to Newgate and cross over to the wonderfully-named St Sepulchre-without-Newgate church opposite and the church's adjoining watch house in Giltspur Street. On the wall of the watch house is William Reynolds-Stephens' (1935) superb bust of **Charles Lamb 39** (1775-1834), essayist, author and poet. Lamb was a student at Christ's Hospital, a charity school chartered by Edward VI in 1552; the inscription reads: 'Perhaps the most loved name in English literature who was a Bluecoat boy here for seven years.' Continue

Old Bailey

Golden Boy

along Giltspur Street to Cock Lane on the left, where set high up on the wall on the right-hand side is the gilt (wood) cherub the **Golden Boy of Pye Corner** 40 , marking the spot where the Great Fire was stopped in 1666.

Return to St Sepulchre and go right along Holborn Viaduct, cross over and go left down Fleet Place to see Stephen Cox's monolithic sculpture **Echo** 41 , consisting of two giant stone male and female torsos, located outside the City Thameslink station since 1993. Outside number 10 Fleet Place is Eilis O'Connor's **Zuni-Zennor** 42 , comprising three sinuous steel elements that combine to form a wave-like effect. Return

to Holborn Viaduct (see box) and continue west to the viaduct itself, which has some exquisite gilded metalwork and is adorned with a number of statues. On the bridge are four bronze allegorical statues, **Science and Fine Art** 43 by William Farmer and William Brindley on the north side, and Henry Bursill's **Commerce and Agriculture** 44 on the south side. At the ends of the bridge are pairs of bronze winged lions by Farmer and Brindley.

Holborn Viaduct figures

The four Renaissance-style pavilions at each end of the viaduct were built to house steps from the viaduct to Farringdon Street below. The two pavilions on the north side were badly damaged in the Second World War and were rebuilt in 2001 (western) and 2014 (eastern). These have carved Neptune heads over the lower arches and a balcony on each side supported by bearded, scowling, male half-figures (atlantes). Each building houses a single carved stone statue of a former Lord Mayor of the City of London. On the south side is **Sir Henry fitz Ailwin** 45 (ca. 1135-1212), London's first Lord Mayor, and **Sir**

Holborn Viaduct

Designed by City surveyor William Haywood and built by engineer Rowland Mason Ordish, the viaduct was constructed in 1863-1869, spanning the steep-sided Holborn Hill and the River Fleet valley. A road bridge – 1,400ft (430m) long and 80ft (24m) wide – the viaduct consists of a cast-iron girder bridge with three spans on granite piers. It was one of London's first modern flyovers.

Monument to Chancery Lane

Thomas Gresham **46**, both by Henry Bursill. Above the northwest steps on the western building is a copy of Bursill's original statue of **Sir William Walworth 47** (died 1385), twice Lord Mayor and the slayer of Peasants' Revolt leader, Wat Tyler. The recently rebuilt eastern pavilion houses a statue of **Sir Hugh Myddleton 48** (1560-1631), engineer and entrepreneur.

Insurance Company (now a conference centre). In the centre of the road is Albert Toft's **Royal Fusiliers War Memorial 51**, dedicated to the 22,000 soldiers of the Royal Fusiliers (City of London Regiment) who died in the First World War. Erected in 1922, the 8½ft (2½m) bronze portrays a fusilier in service dress with rifle and fixed bayonet, mounted on a 16½ft (5m) Portland stone pedestal.

Just past the statue you come to Chancery Lane tube station, which marks the end of the walk. If you're in need of refreshments, **Caffè Vergnano 52** opposite the tube station is located in Tudor Staple Inn, which dates back to 1585 and is one of the few buildings to survive the Great Fire.

Prince Albert

Continue westwards down Holborn Viaduct, where around 200m along in Holborn Circus is Charles Bacon's 1874 equestrian bronze of **Prince Albert 49** (1819-1861). The statue depicts a jaunty Albert in Field Marshal's uniform raising his hat in salute, mounted on a red granite plinth. A short distance past Albert's statue on the right is **De Vere Holborn Bars 50**, a striking Gothic Revival red-brick building built in the 1870s as the HQ of the Prudential

De Vere Holborn Bars

1 The Paternoster	**14** The Gardener
2 Sir Rowland Hill	**15** Shakespeare
3 Memorial to Heroic Self Sacrifice	**16** Guildhall
4 Smithfield Market	**17** Guildhall Art Gallery
5 Memorial to the Peasants' Revolt of 1381	**18** Beyond Tomorrow
6 Sir William Wallace	**19** Glass Fountain
7 St Bartholomew the Great	**20** Anthologist Bar & Restaurant
8 Cloth Fair	**21** Ritual
9 Museum of London	**22** Electra House
10 London Wall Bar & Kitchen	**23** Finsbury Circus Garden
11 Union (Horse with Two Discs)	**24** Britannic House
12 Aldersgate Flame	**25** Bellerophon Taming Pegasus
13 Unity	**26** Rush Hour

● Places of Interest   Food & Drink

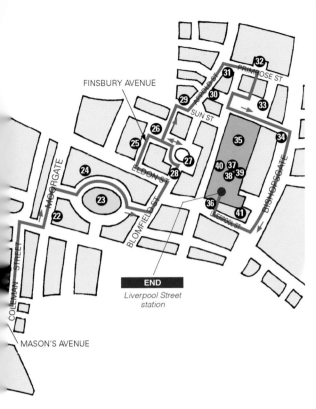

FINSBURY AVENUE

PRIMROSE ST

SUN ST

FINSBURY AVENUE

MOORGATE

ELDON ST

BLOMFIELD ST

COLEMAN STREET

BISHOPSGATE

LIVERPOOL ST

END
*Liverpool Street
station*

MASON'S AVENUE

Smithfield to Liverpool Street

Distance: 3 miles (5 km)
Terrain: easy
Duration: 2 hours
Start: St Paul's tube
End: Liverpool Street tube/rail
Postcode: EC2V 6AA

SMITHFIELD TO LIVERPOOL STREET

This walk takes you across the City of London, from Smithfield in the west to Liverpool Street in the east. Smithfield is drenched in history (and blood) – it has been a meat and livestock market for almost 1,000 years and was a site of public execution in the Middle Ages. It contains a number of monuments and memorials and is home to some venerable buildings, including St Bartholomew's Hospital, St Bartholomew the Great (London's oldest surviving church), Smithfield Market and the 14th-century Charterhouse (almshouse and school).

From Smithfield the route takes in the City's oldest street and visits the Museum of London, before heading east along London Wall, named after the Romans' defensive wall. After a brief excursion to the 15th-century Guildhall, the City's administrative and ceremonial HQ, we go northeast to Finsbury Circus Garden and Broadgate.

It will come as no surprise that the City is rich in historic memorials and sculptures, but most people are unaware that it's also home to a wealth of contemporary sculpture. Nowhere is this more so than in the largely pedestrianised Broadgate development, where sculptures are an integral part of the public amenities. The walk concludes at Liverpool Street Station, itself home to some charming works of art.

Smithfield Market

Smithfield to Liverpool Street

Start Walking…

From St Paul's tube station, take exit 2 and if you want to start with breakfast/brunch, **The Paternoster** 1 in Paternoster Square (approached down Panyer Alley and Paternoster Row) is a good choice. To start your walk, cross Newgate Street and bear right down King Edward Street opposite, where around halfway down on the left, outside the old Post Office HQ, is Edward Onslow Ford's 1884 bronze of **Sir Rowland Hill** 2 (1795-1879), who founded the penny post in

Sir Rowland Hill

1840. Cross the road and enter Postman's Park (see box) – the name reflects its popularity with postal workers – to see the **Memorial to Heroic Self Sacrifice** 3, along with a monument to its creator, the artist, sculptor and philanthropist George Frederic Watts (1817-1904).

Return to King Edward Street, turn right and then bear left into Little Britain, keeping to the side of St Bart's Hospital. At the end is West Smithfield opposite **Smithfield Market** 4, the city's last remaining wholesale market, trading in meat (scheduled to close and become the new Museum of London in 2022). The current building – designed by Sir Horace Jones and opened in 1868 – has some striking statues

Postman's Park

LEIGH PITT.
REPROGRAPHIC OPERATOR
AGED 30, SAVED A DROWNING
BOY FROM THE CANAL AT
THAMESMEAD, BUT SADLY
WAS UNABLE TO SAVE
HIMSELF · JUNE · 7 · 2007

Occupying three old burial grounds, Postman's Park has been a public garden since 1880. It's best known for its Memorial to Heroic Self Sacrifice which commemorates ordinary people who died saving the lives of others. It comprises a series of plaques on a wall beneath a loggia, recording heart-rending acts of selfless sacrifice: rescues from burning buildings, sinking ships and runaway horses. Reading them is an inspiring and humbling experience.

(look for the bronze dragons), decorative stone- and iron-work.

For more than 400 years Smithfield was also a place of public execution, where heretics, rebels and criminals were burnt, beheaded or boiled! Over 200 Protestants were burnt at the stake here during the reign of Queen 'Bloody' Mary alone. As you leave Little Britain, immediately on the left on the wall of St Bart's is Emily Hoffnung's 2015 **Memorial to the Peasants' Revolt of 1381** 5; a protest by thousands of peasants against punitive taxes, it fizzled out when the Lord Mayor of London, William Walworth, stabbed rebel leader Wat Tyler to death. A little further along on the same wall is a memorial to Scottish hero **Sir William Wallace** 6 (1270-1305), who was hanged, drawn and quartered here for high treason. Wallace was one of the leaders during the Wars of Scottish Independence, who famously defeated an English army at the Battle of Stirling Bridge in 1297.

St Bartholomew the Great

A priory church was first established here in 1123 as part of a monastery of Augustinian canons and the site has been in continuous use as a place of worship ever since. With its rich history, interesting architecture, artworks and interior features, it's well worth the price of admission (£5).

Return to Little Britain where, just before Cloth Fair, is the entrance to one of the City's oldest churches, **St Bartholomew the Great 7** (see box). The church and its surroundings – including the lovely medieval gate surmounted by a half-timbered Tudor building – are adorned with a number of statues. On the gatehouse, there's a war memorial in the form of Christ on the cross to the right of the entrance, and a statue of St Bartholomew above, both dating from 1917; a statue of 12th-century Prior Rahere from 1893 adorns the West Porch, overlooking the church path, and another effigy of St Bartholomew from the same year stands above the North Porch. All four were sculpted by William Silver Frith.

On leaving the church turn right into **Cloth Fair 8**, the City's oldest street, where in medieval times merchants gathered to buy and sell cloth during the annual Bartholomew Fair. Numbers 41 & 42 are the oldest residential dwellings in London, while tucked around the corner in Cloth Court is number 43, the former home of poet John Betjeman. Continue along Cloth Fair into Middle Street, turn left at the end and then go right along Long Lane. At the end turn right along Aldersgate Street and head south to the Rotunda and the **Museum of London 9**, which is free to explore but needs at least half a day to do it justice. If you're ready for lunch, the **London Wall Bar & Kitchen 10** next door serves pizzas, burgers and salads.

Climb up to the High Walk where outside the entrance to the museum is a cast of Christopher Le Brun's huge bronze, **Union (Horse with Two Discs) 11** from 2000. In the same location is the **Aldersgate Flame 12**, a vast abstract bronze by Martin Ludlow (1981). It commemorates the conversion of John Wesley (1703-1791), founder of Methodism, which took place in 1738 close to this spot; Wesley's description of his experience is reproduced on the memorial.

Union (Horse with Two Discs)

London Wall

This busy street is named after the wall built by the Romans in the late 2nd or early 3rd century AD. Constructed from Kentish ragstone, it was one of the largest projects undertaken in Roman Britain: 2 miles (3.2km) long, 8ft (2.5m) wide and up to 16ft (5m) high, with five gates (two more were added later), 22 towers and a defensive ditch 16ft (5m) wide. Remnants of the wall can still be seen around the City.

From the museum head east along London Wall (see box) to number 125, aka Alban Gate, a Postmodernist building designed by Sir Terry Farrell, where the atrium is the setting for Croatian sculptor Ivan Klapez's 1992 bronze **Unity** ⓭, depicting nude male and female dancers on a triangular base. Continue along London Wall and go right into Brewers' Hall Gardens to see Karin Jonzen's roughly-finished statue **The Gardener** ⓮, commissioned in 1971. From the gardens, go left on Aldermanbury Square and right on Aldermanbury to lovely St Mary Aldermanbury Garden on the right. Here you see Charles John Allen's bust of **Shakespeare** ⓯ which commemorates not William Shakespeare himself but two of his King's Men acting troupe, John Heminges (1556-1630) and Henry Condell (1576-1627), both of whom are buried at St Mary's,

After the Bard's death in 1616, the pair collected his plays and published them (as the *First Folio*) at their own expense. Without them, Shakespeare's works might have been lost for ever!

From the garden, continue south along Aldermanbury and go left past St Lawrence Jewry church to Guildhall Piazza via Guildhall Yard. The magnificent **Guildhall** ⓰ was completed in 1440 and is the only surviving non-ecclesiastical stone building in the City from this period. To the right of the Guildhall is the superb **Guildhall Art Gallery** ⓱ (free), which houses the collection of the City of London and also provides access to the remains of a Roman amphitheatre discovered in 1988. Within the arcade frontage are four stone busts in niches (from left to right): Sir Christopher Wren, William Shakespeare, Oliver Cromwell and Samuel Pepys – all sculpted by Tim Crawley and dating from 1999 – while next to Pepys, at the north end of the arcade, is Laurence Tyndall's stone three-quarter relief of four-time Lord Mayor Richard Whittington, complete with cat.

Guildhall

In the north of the Piazza is another Karin Jonzen bronze, **Beyond Tomorrow** ⓲, which was donated to the City of London in 1972. It depicts two naked figures, male and female, reclining and looking northwards. Also outside the Guildhall is Allen David's (1969) striking green **Glass Fountain** ⓳. From Guildhall Piazza go left on Gresham Street where, opposite, on the corner of Ironmonger Lane, is **The Anthologist 20**, a deli, bar and restaurant. Take the next left down Basinghall Street and after around 100m turn right along Masons Avenue to Coleman Street, where you go left. On the left outside the Woolgate Exchange in White Horse Yard is Antanas Braždys' stainless-steel sculpture **Ritual** ㉑, an abstract work dating from 1969.

Ritual

Continue to the end of Coleman Street, past the Girdlers' Company livery hall on the left and on to London Wall. Turn right and at the crossroads, cross over London Wall to the eastern side of Moorgate, where on the right at number 84 is **Electra House** ㉒. It was designed by John Belcher and built in 1903 as the HQ of the Eastern Telegraph and Allied Companies (later Cable & Wireless); during the Second World War it was the office of Department EH (part of the Special Operations Executive) and is now part of London Metropolitan University. The building is adorned with decorative sculptures at various levels, which contain many fine works by artists from the New Sculpture movement, including George Frampton, Alfred Drury and Frederick William Pomeroy.

Finsbury Circus Garden

London's oldest public park (8am to dusk) dates from the early 1600s, when Moor Fields (as it was then known) was drained and planted with trees. At 5.4 acres (2.2ha) it's also the City's largest park. The name comes from its elliptical shape, which resembles a Roman 'circus'; it's noted for its mature London plane trees (some over 200 years old), a fine Japanese pagoda tree, and its 1925 bowling green and bandstand. In recent years it has been largely taken over by the Crossrail project, due for completion in 2019, when the garden will be restored to its former glory.

From Electra House continue north on Moorgate and go right along Finsbury Circus to **Finsbury Circus Garden** ㉓ (see box). In the northwest corner of the Circus is Sir Edwin Lutyens' magnificent **Britannic House** ㉔, built

Britannic House

Food & Drink

1 **The Paternoster:** Close to St Paul's Cathedral in Paternoster Square, this modern, glass-fronted Young's pub delivers a hearty breakfast/brunch (Mon-Fri 8am-11pm, Sat-Sun 10am-11pm, £).

10 **London Wall Bar & Kitchen:** Next door to the Museum of London, this Benugo outlet serves wood-fired pizzas, burgers and fresh salads, plus a range of craft beers and wines (Mon-Fri 8am-9/10/11pm, £).

20 **The Anthologist:** Bar-deli-restaurant serving everything from cocktails to cheeseburgers, flatbreads and fries (Mon-Fri 7.30am-11pm/midnight, £-££).

41 **Hamilton Hall**: A luxurious (but noisy) pub serving Wetherspoon's usual good beers and pub grub (Mon-Sat 7am-11.30pm, Sun 9am-10.30pm, £).

Woman and Baby, Persian Scarf Dancer, Indian Water Carrier and Britannia with Trident. Continue clockwise around the Circus and exit in the east to Blomfield Street, turn left and follow the road around to Eldon Street and go right on Finsbury Avenue. A short way up on the left is American Jacques Lipchitz's 1977 bronze of **Bellerophon Taming Pegasus 25** , an imposing 23-tonne work depicting the Greek hero Bellerophon wrestling the winged horse Pegasus, poised precariously on its slender pedestal. Continue along Finsbury Avenue to Finsbury Avenue Square – in the huge Broadgate (see box, page 183) development – and American George Segal's mid-'80s bronze **Rush Hour 26** , depicting a group of miserable-looking commuters heading home. After dark the square is transformed into a kaleidoscope of colours, courtesy of 100,000 LED lights set into the hard landscaping, which produce ten different striking displays.

Rush Hour

Return to Finsbury Square, go east to Broadgate Circle and walk clockwise round to the southeast side to see Barry Flanagan's 1988 sculpture, **Leaping Hare on Crescent and Bell 27** . A recurring theme in Flanagan's work, the hare often poses as if human, playing musical

1921-25. It contains a number of freestanding architectural sculptures on the second floor of its Circus frontage by Francis Derwent Wood; from left to right,

Ceramic Sculpture

instruments, dancing, boxing, leaping, performing acrobatics or interacting with technology. From the Circle take the path south to Octagon Mall to see Richard Serra's vast 55ft (17m) **Fulcrum** 28 , a wigwam-like steel structure that gives the viewer the illusion that the five sheets of steel are simply leaning against one another. From the Fulcrum retrace your steps to Finsbury Avenue Square and take the footpath in the northeast corner past the Broadgate Welcome Centre. Here you see David Batchelor's **Chromorama** 29 , a totemic sculpture containing 35 illuminated light boxes in a spectrum of colours facing in all directions.

Broadgate Venus

Turn right on Sun Street and follow it around to Appold Street, where you find Catalan Xavier Corberó's (1991) sculpture, **The Broad Family** 30 – represented by a cluster of basalt rocks – at the entrance to Exchange Square on the right. Continue along Appold Street and turn right on Primrose Street, where on the right-hand corner is Spanish artist Joan Gardy Artigas' (1990) **Ceramic Sculpture** 31 , a bright, hand-painted tiled work that soars several stories skywards. A short way along Primrose Street (on the left in front of Broadgate Tower) is Stephen Cox's 1988 work, **Ganapathi and Devi** 32 , a monumental two-part abstract granite sculpture. It portrays the female Hindu goddess Devi set alongside a second stone of Ganapathi, the South Indian name for the popular elephant god Ganesha.

From Ganapathi and Devi, ascend the stairs opposite to Exchange Square, where on the left-hand side is Colombian artist Fernando Botero's 5-tonne bronze **Broadgate Venus** 33 , installed in 1989. Featuring the artist's signature enlarged 'Picasso-esque' forms, with generous proportions and rolling curves, it's one of Botero's largest sculptures. To the right of Venus is a striking Japanese-inspired water feature by Stephen Cox and architects Skidmore, Owings & Merrill.

From Exchange Square, follow the path east to Bishopsgate to see Bruce McLean's (1993) towering sculpture **Eye-I** 34 , an abstract witty 'sketch' of a face made from brightly coloured strips of steel. Walk south along Bishopsgate to Liverpool Street and the main entrance to **Liverpool Street Station** 35 – London's third-busiest after

Smithfield to Liverpool Street

Broadgate

A 32-acre (13ha) office and retail estate, Broadgate was the largest office development in London until Canary Wharf in the early '90s. The mainly pedestrianised development is located on the original site of Broad Street Station (closed in 1986) and beside and above the railway approaches to Liverpool Street Station. It houses an impressive public art collection by British and international artists, including sculptures in bronze, ceramic, steel and stone.

Waterloo and Victoria – where there are a number of interesting memorials and sculptures.
In Hope Square, just outside the station entrance, is Frank Meisler's sculpture, **Children of the Kindertransport** ㊱ , aka Kindertransport – The Arrival. The 2006 statue is dedicated to the Jewish children who fled Nazi persecution in 1938-1939 and found refuge in Britain, via the gateway of Liverpool Street Station.

Enter the station and go right, where on the left on the east wall is Charles Leonard Hartwell's (1923) memorial plaque to Field Marshal **Sir Henry Wilson** ㊲ (1864-1922), Chief of the Imperial General Staff from 1918; to its right is H.T.H. van Goldberdinge's 1917 memorial to **Captain Charles Fryatt** ㊳ (1872-1916), captain of the SS Brussels, who was executed by the Germans for attempting to ram a U-Boat in 1915. Above the two plaques is the **Great Eastern Railway War Memorial** ㊴ by

architectural sculptors Farmer and Brindley (1922). Return to the stairs and descend to the lower floor, where (on the right) to the left of the entrance to the underground station, is another statue commemorating the Kindertransport: Flor Kent's (2003) touching bronze sculpture **Für Das Kind** ㊵ (For the Children), depicting two forlorn-looking children with suitcases.

The station marks the end of the walk. If you fancy a drink or a bite to eat you're spoilt for choice, but if it's a pint you're after, Wetherspoon's **Hamilton Hall** 41 – named after Lord Claud Hamilton (1843-1925), former chairman of the Great Eastern Railway Company – in the gilded former ballroom of the Great Eastern Hotel, is a cut above your average boozer.

Children of the Kindertransport

London's Architectural Walks
Jim Watson

ISBN: 978-1-909282-85-8, 128 pages, softback, £9.99

London's Architectural Walks is a unique guide to the most celebrated landmark buildings in one of the world's major cities. In thirteen easy walks, it takes you on a fascinating journey through London's diverse architectural heritage with historical background and clear maps. Some of the capital's most beautiful parks are visited, plus palaces, theatres, museums and some surprising oddities. With the author's line and watercolour illustrations of all the city's significant buildings, *London's Architectural Walks* is an essential companion for anyone interested in the architecture that has shaped this great metropolis.

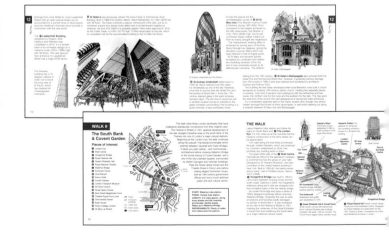

INDEX

185

T

U/V

W

X/Y

Z

London's Secret Walks, 2nd edition
Graeme Chesters

ISBN: 978-1-909282-93-3, 320 pages, softback, £10.99

London is a great city for walking – whether for pleasure, exercise or simply to get from A to B. The inspiration for this book was Samuel Johnson's advice to his friend Boswell in the 18th century, on the occasion of the latter's arrival in London: "survey its innumerable little lanes and courts." By extension, wander off the beaten tourist track and you'll find a world of fascinating sights, as you would expect in a city as large and old as London.

London's Green Walks
David Hampshire

ISBN: 978-1-909282-82-7, 192 pages, softback, £9.99

Green spaces cover almost 40 per cent of Greater London, ranging from magnificent royal parks and garden cemeteries, full of intrigue and history, to majestic ancient forests and barely tamed heathland; from elegant squares and formal country parks to enchanting 'secret' gardens. Our twenty walks take in famous destinations, such as Hyde Park and Regent's Park, but also many smaller and lesser known – but no less beautiful – parks and gardens, all of which are free to explore.

London's Village Walks
David Hampshire

ISBN: 978-1-909282-94-0, 192 pages, softback, £9.99

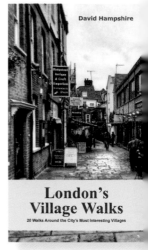

Unlike more modern cities, London wasn't planned logically but grew organically. From its beginnings as a Roman trading port some 2,000 years ago, it has mushroomed into the metropolis we see today, swallowing up thousands of villages, hamlets and settlements in the process. Nevertheless, if you're seeking a village vibe you can still find it if you know where to look. Scratch beneath the surface of modern London and you'll find a rich tapestry of ancient villages, just waiting to be rediscovered.

London's Village Walks explores 20 of the city's most interesting and best preserved 'villages', where – with a little imagination – it's still possible to picture yourself living in a bygone age.